Ripples on the Water

Memories from eighty years of shooting and fishing

by
Peter Arnold

Compiled and edited by
Tom O'Connor

Ripples on the Water

Published 2020
by Peter Arnold

ISBN 978-0-57-868285-3

Designed by:
Real Graphic
749 Maltman Drive
Grass Valley, CA 95945

DEDICATION

*This work is dedicated to Sarah
with love and so many thanks for
our long life together*

TABLE OF CONTENTS

ACKNOWLEDGMENTS

First and foremost, thanks again to Tom O'Connor, the brains and the drive behind getting this book together. It never would have happened without you. So, many thanks good friend.

To Robert Douglas of Waikanae, New Zealand, for such a great job of getting this work ready for print. Also many thanks.

To my very favorite cousin Serafina Bathrick, in faraway Sicily, and to my dearest niece Jean Arnold, who between them edited, proofed, and corrected my writing with such patient and gimlet eyes. How lucky I am to have relatives like you!

To Jennifer Schrader of Real Graphics, for her patient forbearance in getting this to press.

To August Brooks, for his wizardry at the keyboard to tame my word processor and his valuable suggestions for editing changes.

To Steve and Larry Marvier who took me on my last duck hunt on a public hunting ground.

To John Karlonas who hosted Tony and me on so many goose, duck, dove, and turkey hunts for so many years.

To David Barale, not only for wonderful hunts in the past, but also for my most recent and perhaps last stay in a duck blind.

To so many more people who deserve individual mention, who I was not able to include here.

And finally, to all you who have so encouraged me to write. You cannot know how much your support has meant to me.

PREFACE

This book would never have seen the light of day were it not for Tom O'Connor, a noted New Zealand author and journalist. It is as much his as mine and I consider it ours.

We first met when he came to California on a hunter exchange program my late brother Tony had set up, and we had hit it off together.

We continued to stay in touch with emails off and on, but in the last couple of years the correspondence faltered and a blank ensued.

One day, a year ago, I decided to get back in touch with him, and sent an email together with a short work on hunting I had written. It was one of a number of pieces I had posted on the California Flyway Forum, a gaggle of oddball duck hunters I consort with online. I had also contributed a few of them to the California Waterfowl Association's periodical. I'll never forget Tom's immediate response: "You, sir, are a wordsmith!" ...Pretty high praise from someone as talented as he.

He then asked me to send anything else I had written—he sensed a book could come out of my reminiscence of outdoor experiences.

Friends and relatives had urged me to write a book, but I had never felt my writing was that good. In fact I still don't. But to please Tom, I bundled all the stories of hunting and fishing I had written and fired them off to him.

He selected those he thought worth reading, edited them, and put them together in this book. He also added all too few enjoyable and thoughtful comments and contributions here and there. I wish there were more of them.

Preface

This is not the first time that Tom has gotten himself embroiled with an Arnold and publishing. We can all thank him for two books by two Arnolds.

In 2010 Tony, already an author of five books, had written Tom his thoughts about giving up on duck hunting and writing. Tom had come back with a blistering condemnation of the idea and suggested Tony devote some time to getting another book out.

That Tony did in 2012, with *Spent Shells*, a far larger work than this, and far better written. I feel I have to mention this in order that the reader not think I was trying to outdo my brother. Indeed, his work casts a deep shadow over mine. But heck, he was a professional writer, and a damned good one. Being in that shadow is easy.

Tony continued hunting through the 2015 spring turkey season, bagging a big tom. He died just before the start of the 2015–2016 waterfowl season. Otherwise, knowing Tony, he'd have been in a blind on opening day.

So, reader, thank you for taking the time to read this, and I hope you will derive at least some of the enjoyment that I did in writing these stories.

INTRODUCTION

There are vast ranks of hunting and fishing books for those days, and evenings, when it is not advisable for any man, or woman for that matter, of average intelligence and survival instincts to venture out into the tempest in search of prey. There are also those beautiful bluebird days when the combined risks of sunstroke and dehydration outweigh any remote chance of catching some critter unawares. On those times, and in the off season, a good book of someone else's adventures and hard-luck stories makes an easy companion, provided of course another, mortal, companion does not already have a list of essential chores a dusty road mile long to take up any surplus time between waking and sleeping, as they are want to do from time to time.

These squadrons of books then remind us of our own similar adventures and failures and keep alive the primal urge to be afield as soon as all other, more mundane constraints like earning a living, chopping the firewood, or painting the kitchen walls (again) allows. Now and then we might pick up a hint among the pages of a new idea to try; a different shot shell, decoy design, or trout lure which has brought success to the writer might be worth a try next season.

This book however is not one of those even though most of the material it contains was probably written with those things in mind. This book is, unintentionally I believe, a chronicle of some of the most important lessons in hunting skill, knowledge of the vast outdoors and appreciation of nature learned over a very long lifetime of active involvement. It is not just about how to bring birds and fish to bag or how to avoid game wardens intent on enforcing nonsensical laws. This tale follows the development of an intense affection for nature in all her moods from a small boy to man of mature years who has been brave and honorable enough to list his failings and hard lessons along with his successes. These things are timeless in their value to those who take the time to read and commit them to memory.

Pete (as he is known to most) was born in San Francisco on May 10,1924 and grew up in California the fifth of six children of a dedicated hunting and fishing father and indulgent mother. There were three brothers and two sisters who all shared a love of the outdoors to some degree.

Pete still recalls Sunday nights when his father and older brothers would come home with burlap sacks loaded with and smelling of wet ducks. He learned duck identification from the contents of those sacks. He shot his first ducks and doves at 13 and was hooked from there on. Later he used a Remington Model 32 over and under 12 ga and later a Browning of the same configuration.

In his youth he spent three years in the US Navy in World War Two as a pharmacist's mate but saw no action even though he was due on the invasion of Kyushu, Japan towards the end of the war. That war took his older brother Kent in the bloody campaign to take Iwo Jima, a tiny dot in the Pacific, but held tenaciously by the Japanese.

After the war Pete went to Yale University to study for bachelor's and master's degrees in forestry and forest management and he spent fifty years in the profession of forestry, including international projects that provided opportunities to hunt and fish. He spent four years as a forestry advisor to the Government of Ecuador.

Beyond his working life outdoors Pete spent thirteen years on his home county fish and wildlife commission and was awarded an honorable life membership of the California Waterfowl Association. He hunted birds in several states in the US, and Ecuador, but was most active in California, almost entirely in northern California marshes and rice fields.

In retirement Pete planted a small wine grape vineyard and supplied local wineries for 30 years.

Health problems put an end to his regular hunting by 2015, the year his last surviving brother, Tony, died but he has still tried to get out at least once a year. But without a gun.

In retirement he took up writing for his own enjoyment and posted quite a few articles on a California duck hunters' forum and several that have been published in CWA's magazine over the years. Many of those are included here.

This then is the story of Peter Arnold as he treads the sometimes marshy and sometimes stony path of true enlightenment about the natural world and essential role and obligations of hunters and anglers in that world. It is written in his own words over many years for several different publications and sometimes simply for family members and friends. I was privileged to be included in that latter category when I met Peter and his late brother Tony on the hunter-exchange system with New Zealand in 2001.

It took me some time to persuade Pete to allow me to put his writings into a book. I am glad I succeeded.

Tom O'Connor
New Zealand
2020

CHAPTER 1

STARTING AND QUITTING

WHEN TO QUIT

Some years ago the *CWA Magazine* published something I wrote called "When to Quit."

It dealt with duck hunters who had come to the end of their hunting days, voluntarily and involuntarily. I myself was not yet one of them.

But today some five years later, things have changed. My brother's ashes now lie around the duck blinds he loved, so I cannot hunt with that close companion again. Beyond that my own health has begun betraying me, but heck, at closer to 92 than 91, what should I expect?

What I resent is that after all the exercise at the gym and doing stretches at home, I am beset with an ailing heart, the very same one I have carted to the gym all these ten years to give it the exercise it needed. Ungrateful wretch.

As I write this, the 2015–2016 season — the regular duck season, that is — comes to a close at the end of this week. I have been out only once, though I had wonderful plans for hunting the MI (mobile-impaired) blinds of the public hunting grounds, somehow I never got up the energy to drive down all those Wednesday afternoons I thought I would enjoy. Now I have one last opportunity, an invitation in these closing days to hunt a wonderful place with a most pleasant and generous host. Luckily for me he is an EMT, so I shall be in good hands if anything goes wrong with me. But I have a feeling this will be my last duck hunt.

WHEN TO START HUNTING

Maybe you can't start too early, though perhaps there are extremes to be avoided. Long ago a friend took her two two-month-old son to the blind and had to club to death a wounded Canada that had fallen close by. She was worried the bird might attack her offspring, and she beat it to death lest it succeed. For the son, appropriately named Hunter, apparently that was a little early, and Hunter never did take to shooting. (However, his three younger brothers all became really enthusiastic hunters.) I take little pride in describing the first time I went out, aged 7.

My father took me into his big redwood barrel blind, five feet deep, so I sat down in the dark while he shot. It was cold, it was dank, I couldn't see a thing, and I was miserable and I let him know it. I cannot imagine anyone's whining the way I did. We got back at noon, and he didn't take me back after lunch. In fact he didn't invite me to go again for another six years, not until I was 13.

He also held off taking my younger brother Tony until he too reached 13, doubtless fearing the same kind of behavior I had demonstrated. That is too bad, because Tony probably would have been a far more amenable blind companion than I was, but he was cheated out of at least a couple of years of hunting enjoyment because of the way I carried on that day. I can't believe how awful I was.

But there is hope. I took my son on his first duck hunt just before his 6th birthday. We were guests at a blue-ribbon Butte Sink club. A good friend of my uncle's had called two days before pheasant season opened to invite me, but I had to refuse, explaining that I'd promised a small boy I'd take him with me as I opened pheasant season that day at a mutual friend's. "How small a boy?" asked my host, and when I explained, he came back with "Well, that's pretty small — I think he could share a blind with you," and we were on.

We arrived at the club just as the breakfast bell rang. I said, "Come on, or we'll be late!" and Pete whined, "I don't feel very well, I'm not hungry, I've got a stomach ache." And I thought to myself "Appendicitis? Nerves? What?" "OK, you wait here with the dog and I'll come back for you after breakfast," and off I went. When I returned the stomach ache was gone and he was already putting on the little hip boots I'd just bought him. A ten-minute trip by boat in the dark and Phelps dropped the two of us off with the dog at our blind and went to the next. As always at that club it was a great hunt, a limit of greenheads and sprig by mid-morning, and young Peter was sitting where he could watch it all. Phelps finished as well, and we started picking up decoys.

Pete was out there helping me in those absurd little hip boots, and somehow in that shallow water he managed to trip over a decoy line and fall flat on his face. He came up wondering whether to laugh or to cry, and finally decided it really was funny.

That day locked him into duck hunting. From then on I'd take him almost every weekend day I hunted. He loved every minute of the time we spent out there.

The year he reached ten, on the day he got his license I took him to the duck club, armed with the same 20 gauge double I had started with. Shooting time came, four sprig came by and I told him to shoot.

He stood up, aiming the gun as if he was shooting at a stationary target some way in front of him. No swing when he pulled the trigger, no nothing, and the ducks flew on. I told him he had to swing, to start from behind, pulling ahead of the bird, then shoot, never stopping that swing. Next bird, a wigeon, cupped his wings dropped down and swung by in easy range. Same stationary lead, a shot, and he flew away.

Then I put down a bird and went out after it. As I started back, a hen sprig came over me in easy range headed right toward the blind, fifty yards away. "Mark, Pete!" I shouted, and waited for him to shoot. And waited. And waited. Then Blam! That bird looked as if it had flown into a brick wall. Down it went, and our dog shot after it and delivered to him. Pete was stroking the feathers, starry eyed when I got back.

He said, "At first I pointed at it the way I did the others, and then I remembered what you said, so I swung the gun back behind it and then brought it forward and shot as I was swinging. That's what you meant!"

It was as if he had unlocked his eye, for he hit consistently well the rest of the morning and shot his limit.

Then there is Tyler Marvier. His father, Steve, began taking Tyler with him when he was five, later arming him with a bb gun and his own set of calls. Tyler became so accomplished a caller that at a CWA event for juniors he won first prize, a lifetime hunting license, and he was competing with boys a lot older than he. Meanwhile his father one time at Howard Slough hit a greenhead that, still alive, slanted down toward a thick stand of tule. Because Steve didn't have a dog, he shot a second time to finish it on the way down. Tyler also had been aiming at it with his bb gun, and pulled the trigger simultaneously, apparently never hearing Steve's shot at all, and it folded. "I got him! I got him!" Tyler yelled, and when Steve brought the greenhead back it had a band on one leg.

"Gee, my first duck and it has a band!" marveled Tyler.

Steve couldn't wait for Tyler to get licensed either. "When that happens," he used to say, "I won't have to listen to Tyler saying 'Gee Dad, you sure missed that one. It was an easy shot!' Instead I'll be saying 'Gee, Tyler...'". Tyler has had his license for several years now, but I have not been out with him and his dad to see if that is really happening.

So start your kids early, but not too early. Those who act as badly as I did my first trip, send them back to watch Bugs Bunny or the like and hope they shape up. Those who emulate my son or Tyler, they will be your best hunting companions for the rest of your hunting life.

CHAPTER 2

MY FIRST GREENHEAD

How many of us remembers his first duck? I barely do; it was a bird crossing from left to right over the pond, I killed it with one shot, either a GWT or a hen sprig. For the life of me I cannot tell you which.

But as if it were yesterday the memory of my first greenhead sticks in my mind. It was at my father's club on the Suisun Marsh when I was 14 years old.

After lunch at the Arnold Club everyone would go back out to the flooded South Field to hunt from blinds. Sometimes I would head out to the North Field, unflooded but with canals and a slough trapped behind the levee. Mallards used those waterways, almost always in singles and pairs, and I wanted a greenhead in the worst way. I do not remember how many tries it took me to accomplish that goal, but I have a most vivid memory of the first and only one I ever pulled out of the North Field.

Sneaking mallards out there was a catch-as-catch can situation, for I never knew where I might find them. So I would walk along the edge of the narrow canal, partly overgrown with tules. For a small boy packing a 20 gauge side by side, when birds jumped, it was a question of who was the most startled. With a clatter of wings and the hen quacking they would jump in the air, rattling me so badly that invariably I would throw up the gun wildly, maybe even pulling both triggers before it got to my shoulder, and miss every time. Up and off they would go, and that would be my hunt for the afternoon. I do not remember how many times that happened to me, but it was several.

But one day as I was walking along the north beside the bigger slough, suddenly a pair jumped, the drake on the right. I fired both barrels at him, thought I saw him stagger, and go on. Foiled again, I thought, but then to my utter joy he staggered again in flight and then suddenly at about 150 yards, he dropped like a stone. I'd done it! I'd done it! I'd killed a greenhead!

But how to go after him? I could strip down, swim across the 20 yard slough with clothes, gun and boots, dress back up and follow my mark. Or could I do it in one trip? That was a lot of gear. And what if I were to get the gun wet or, worse yet, drop it in the black waters? Or I could avoid the swim and take a quarter mile walk to get to where the slough ended at the railroad track, come back the quarter mile on the other side, a half mile hike with the possibility that I'd never find that duck without the clear mark I had from where I had shot. I elected the walk, but was not at all confident of finding that duck. Probably it had fallen in thick grass, to be found by some marsh hawk or raccoon, not by me.

I got to the point across the slough from where I was pretty sure I had jumped the birds, picked up what I thought was my mark and started walking to it. Soon I was into a burned area, all heavy salt grass matted, black and curly. Out in front of me, right in line with my mark, something different, something unbelievable.

I started running, got to it, and there, lying on his back in that blackened ash, was my first greenhead, a big duck with the reddest of legs, not a mark or even a bead of blood on him. I shall never forget the surge of joy and pride I felt as I picked up that duck and headed back to the clubhouse.

2011 DUCK HUNT

Those of you who read my "When to Quit" article in the CWA mag last summer may remember my writing that perhaps the one greenwing I got last year could very well be my last duck. But no, yesterday, my fifth hunt of 2010–2011, after never connecting, yesterday morning I got one more. Of course I should have done a lot better, but heck, if my limit is going to be one bird a season, I'll be happy with it.

It was a great hunt in the fog with my son and our host. Visibility was maybe a hundred yards, and in the chilly mist, with sky and water indistinguishable from one another, the tule patches around us seemed to be floating in mid-air. Dave had said the night before that if the fog came back we'd be seeing a lot of teal. Indeed we did. By the time we had to quit at about 10:30, Pete and Dave had their limits and I had mine, all teal plus three other drakes — a wigeon, a bluie, and a ring neck.

The birds would appear out of nowhere and just as quickly disappear into the fog, sometimes reappearing to respond to Dave's squeaky hen teal quack, sometimes offering only that one opportunity. That called for a lot faster reaction time than I can handle any more, but it was no problem for those two guys; they were fast and deadly.

Clicker had the time of his life retrieving, and failed on only one bird that dived and must have stayed under. For a dog that gets all too little chance to hunt, he did a great job of marking. If doubles fell far apart, he almost always seemed to remember where they had come down and after retrieving the first he'd make a bee line for the second.

If he didn't see the second bird fall, the command "Back!" with a hand signal was enough to put him on line, and his vision was so keen he'd see the bird even when I couldn't. That was a tired, happy dog, and a proud and happy boss that waded out of that marsh yesterday morning.

What a hunt, what a caller, what a host, what a great cook. Thanks, Dave, that was an unforgettable time!

SECOND DUCK HUNT 2012

Two years ago this magazine published an article I had written, "Time to Quit?" in which I tracked older people who had hung up their guns for one reason or another, and mused about when I might.

This year, as duck season approached its next to last Saturday, my brother and I set, I think, some sort of record: two guys, 83 and 87, going out duck hunting unattended by any youngsters trying to keep us in line. Just imagine, 170 years stuffed into one blind.

Time was we used to paddle out to the blinds in his canoe, a journey sometimes exciting.

Once on opening day his dog swamped us at the edge of deep water trying to get at a jumping bird. We were youngsters then, I only 79 and Tony 75. We righted the canoe, bailed it out, and continued to the blind. But the canoe now sits at home.

This time we drive out in the dark, in style in the club's UTV, almost to the blind itself. As we leave the club and head west, the wind, that cold, cold northwest wind, hits us face on. At least it isn't raining.

We turn off the levee onto the road to the blind, and as we go sense glimpses of dark shapes hurtling into the air — ducks startled by the Kubota's lights. Arrive at the stake marking the blind path, offload the gear, and Tony drives off to hide the buggy while I wait. That northwest wind is whooping it up and in a moment flicks off my parka hood, then my cap, and off it goes. That cap may end up somewhere over in east Yolo County in that gale. I'll likely never see it again. I am lucky to have a good insulated hood on my jacket, so just pull the strings on it to keep my head covered.

Tony trudges back to me in the still dark, his dog Shade alerting me by her arrival. I hand him his gun and ski pole, take mine, and we wade in. We move slowly, testing the bottom, measuring our progress maybe not in feet per minute, but more like minutes per foot, but we do make it to the blind. Pull each square blind cover off and drop it in the water.

Then to the first of the two most prolonged activities which those our age get involved in while duck hunting: entering the blind. (Exiting is the second). Nimbleness is no part of it as one foot searches blindly for the stool below. Ah, there it is. Now step two, getting the other foot up over the lip of the blind. Bend the knee lift, the foot to clear — no, higher than that or you won't make it. Can't make it. Shift a bit, get the knee flexed better, lift — ah, just made it.

Already it is growing light out there, the sun still well below the horizon, the last of the old moon just the slightest sliver of itself. The sky is clear, most of it, but for a layer of dark cloud still hanging over the distant Sierra, and rain squalls behind us. Fifteen minutes to shooting time, and we already see birds. Overhead the sky is still so dark that ducks are not much more than darker blobs, appearing and then quickly disappearing, totally unidentifiable, some only yards up. Ten minutes to shooting time; already we see birds more easily. Even without the wind's constant battering, even with these two pairs of ears equipped with hearing aids, neither of us can any longer hear the whisper of wings, the muted quacks, the whistles of sprig, wigeon or teal, or the occasional overheard scuffle of colliding wings. We can only hark back to when we could. I load my gun.

Five minutes to shooting time and someone can't stand it. Shots ring out upwind. More follow immediately, and by shooting time they are all over the marsh. We have not yet pulled a trigger, not so much because we are so law-abiding but because of no opportunity.

We wait, scanning the sky.

My First Greenhead

I sit with my back to the wind in the western half of the blind, looking east, the hood of my hunting jacket keeping the wind off my neck.

Tony sits downwind of me with only a cap and his face mask protecting him. Drops of rain spit against my hood, and I am thankful not to be looking into the wind.

A few seconds and suddenly Tony pulls up his gun, fires one shot at a bunch of birds that come out of nowhere and just as suddenly go back to nowhere — all but one, and it comes down hard. "What is it?" I ask. "A wigeon, I think," he answers, and stands up. The wind grabs his deer stalker cap and it disappears over the side of the blind. He curses, then sends Shade after the duck. Instead of a wigeon she comes back with a beautiful cock sprig — his first in some years, he says. We are not skunked, but Tony is hatless.

It is now light enough to see how the birds are flying. Most are to the south of us, beating eastward into the wind, some of them low, some high. None is working the decoys of this pond. There is no lee here for birds to seek protection from that never-ending wind, so there is all too little to attract them.

Looking into the brightening dawn we see ducks only as black silhouettes, nothing else. Even the birds to the south of us seem to lack color, so the only way to identify them is by profile, the blockiness of mallards, the long tail of the drake sprig, the wedgey tail look of wigeon.

And of course the small size of the teal and their total abandon in flight. We see a very few Canadas, and they are far up in the sky. Once a pair of ruddies rockets downwind just over the blind. Lucky that neither of us happens to stand up just then, or they'd likely knock a head off or bore a hole right through us.

So any chance we may have will be a passing shot. I take one at a wigeon about 30 yards out and 15 yards up. I don't swing or lead well enough and the shot goes wild. The startled wigeon puts down his flaps, the wind hits them, and lifts that duck a good 30 yards in the blink of an eye. I never had a chance with a second shot, and that was the only opportunity I took all morning.

Tony gets himself out of the blind to go collect a sack of wigeon decoys he's left on the road way, and finds his hat floating on the water in the lee of the blind. He picks it up, shakes it, puts it back on his head, mumbles something about "cooling the fevered brow," and goes for the sack. Returns, puts out the decoys and does the nimble dance of re-entering the blind. Now they are in place we are sure to see some action, aren't we? No, not necessarily.

The birds continue to pass, one side or the other, but almost never overhead in range, and none paying attention.

Tony sticks his head above the blind, the wind nips at his deer stalker, rips it off again. He leans over, pulls it out of the water. shakes it off and puts it back on. That happens at least four times before we finish. His fevered brow definitely gets cooled that morning. I tell him he should glue two Velcro straps, one on his balding pate, the other on the inside of the cap. My humor eludes him.

Ordinarily, club custom is to come in for belated breakfast at about 9:30, but there was consensus this morning that, with all this wind, and all the birds that must be going to be buzzing us, we'd hold off for another hour or two, to take advantage of the promising duck bonanza before coming back. So 9:30 comes and goes, Tony's having fired in vain at three or four more ducks.

Then duck drought sets in for Blind #5, no birds coming any closer than 200, maybe 300 yards. Ten o'clock comes. No ducks, and one of the hunters heads for the club house. Ten thirty comes. No ducks. I'd be happy to roll up the rug, but Tony says, "I'd like to hang in there a little longer." Who am I to say? I am just a guest.

My First Greenhead

Eleven o'clock and Tony pulls out his cell phone to call Bill, who along with him has the breakfast duty, to find out if Bill (a) is yet back and if so, (b) needs help in the kitchen. Bill answers, but Tony can't hear him, so hands the phone to me. Bill says he needs no help, and tells me to sit it out and enjoy the shooting. I hand the phone back to Tony, lie in my teeth, and say yes, he does need help.

So we haul the combined 170 years out of the blind, each of us finding a new and different way of negotiating this increasingly difficult task. Tony goes off to get the Kubota while I put the blind lids back on.

I remember that the lid handle of mine is on top, and my hand searches that frigid water for it. Ah, there it is. Pull it up, shake it off, place it. Find Tony's, upside down, catch a corner and lift. It surfaces, I flip it over, position it. Both lids on, and then I remember my gun sling is still down there. I have to make one more entry, one more exit, but I manage. The lid goes back on, I put the sling on the gun and the gun on my back, grab my poles, and walk back out to the road. How nice that hard bottom feels.

I get to the road and there, a foot from the water, is my cap that had flown off in the dark. I pick it up and watch Tony slowly turn the Kubota and start in my direction. A mental sigh of relief that we don't have to walk the two miles back to the club. The wind pushes sideways on the Kubota, and I see Tony fighting the wheel, the vehicle actually crabbing as it approaches. Its tires are huge, the sticky peat clinging to them. I climb on board and we head for the barn.

I was not conscious of being cold out there, not with four layers on my upper body and heavy neoprene waders, but as we step into the warmth of the kitchen I suddenly realize what it is like to be comfortable. And now a hot cup of coffee is warming my inner self as well. Ah luxury!

So this hunt ends. The duck strap is lighter than I'd like, but the shared time has been rich, very rich. I hope we can do it again. Thanks, younger brother!

ANOTHER DUCK HUNT 2012

This is a story about yet another of my 2012 duck hunts. I must admit that I am partial to the kind of a hunting day out in the blind that, eventually, shows results. Results like at least one, or maybe even a couple of round, well-fed ducks coming roaring and spitting out of the oven, the fat in their skins rendered out and the meat beautifully rare; that is a fine and fitting thing for me, and my wife and I always say "Thank you, duck!" as we make that first slice along the breastbone.

On the other hand I am finding myself less and less disappointed if the day yields no ducks at all to put in the oven. And that has happened to me every time I have hunkered down in a blind this season. I am hopeful that, when and where Spec and I are guests this coming week, maybe I'll at least get my annual teal, as our host has all but promised me. But if not, karma, neh? as our Japanese friends like to say. We are going to be out there to enjoy the day, in a waterfowl habitat that can't be beat.

Two generations before me and many of you who are reading this, men went hunting for the sole purpose of getting food on the table or to get money for what they killed. Sure, well-heeled people even back in the mid-nineteenth century and into the twentieth hunted for fun, but I'd bet that the bag of subsistence and market hunters far exceeded theirs.

Today those well-heeleds are still there, but most of us water fowlers here in CA, some of them relentless women hunters like Holly Heyser, aren't all that wealthy. We hunt ducks not for subsistence; we do it for enjoyment, in the hopes that there will be at least a couple of ducks for the table. But if a hunting day ends without anything on the game strap, it is not the end of the world for any of us. We aren't going to see our kids starve as a result. Of course it can be a real disappointment for some, though, especially to those worrying that the tail gate has no birds to photograph. That graphic but silent boast ain't there, is it?.

So what did I get instead of ducks for the oven yesterday? I got to see a dramatic sunrise I never see at home, even though I am up well before dawn every day. There was the dark blue of the sky directly above, shading off to orange along the Sierra in the distance. As the blind and the marsh hurtled eastward they lifted the sun, first only a slightly rounded brilliant gold strip, peeking over the mountains, then a quarter, then a half, then full. I got to see formless black blobs appear over my head and as quickly disappear — ducks and maybe mudhens passing over in range and gone into the dark.

I got to sit in a blind surrounded by tules, all standing since no one had shot it this season. I got to watch a marsh wren work its way along a tule stem, pecking away at invisible insects. I got to be bombarded by blackbirds using the tules as a way stop.

I got to watch and to listen to stilts flying and landing around us.

I got to hear — even with my poor hearing these days — a huge and riotous gang of swans off to the east of us whooping up a storm of bleats and whistles. Sounded like a great party.

I got to watch my dog race out 75 yards to a crippled sprig which, when he got there, dove on him. Click started spinning round and round in one spot to see if he could spot any movement on the pond's surface that would give the duck away. He saw it, leapt and stuck his head underwater, grabbed it and came galloping back, proud and happy.

I got to watch him do another retrieve, this one of a spoonie the next blind had shot and folded close to it. All my buzzes on his e-collar to bring him back were in vain, (battery was dead and I didn't know it) and he did the distance with a perfect mark, scooped up the bird and galloped back as rapidly as he'd gone out. How can you shoot without a dog to enjoy? Or to see how the dog enjoys himself?

I got to spend time in the blind with a good friend I have known for over forty years. We started hunting together back then, and over those years have shared a lot of hunts, some productive, some not, but all enjoyable. I got to watch him pull on the drake of a pair of sprig, knock it, and let the hen fly on.

I got to watch pintail courting flights, some as few as five birds, some as many as a dozen as they rose, dove, looped and careened about the marsh, never anywhere near in range of us.

I got to watch a manic flight of well over a hundred snow geese, with a couple of darks included, as they came by first headed south and then, for whatever goosely reason, turn north again and go by — but not over us — some 60 yards up, yelling and screeching at each other and, who knows, maybe at us.

So there's all those I-gots, and they were pretty darn good ones for a morning on the marsh.

A duck coming out of the oven would have been nice though…

My First Greenhead

CHAPTER 3

EMILY'S TROUT

There is a stretch of Lake Tahoe's east shore that is too unforgiving to allow development. Its sparsely timbered slopes fall steeply to the lake shore. We were fortunate in having access to one of the only camping areas together with a small beach from which to launch boats.

Otherwise the rest of that stretch of lake shore is uninhabitable.

Large to huge granite boulders line the water's edge for several miles along the shore and extend beneath the surface, sometimes for a short distance but sometimes in reefs out into deep water. Those underwater boulders provide habitat for fish — minnows, chubs, suckers, trout— as well as abundant crayfish introduced into the lake over a hundred years ago.

Tahoe up until the late 1800's had only one trout species, its huge Lahontan cutthroat trout. For many years the cutthroat supplied a thriving fishery and its catch was shipped out to many destinations. Then someone introduced the mackinaw trout (actually a char) and in a remarkably short time it exterminated the native cutthroat, consuming all the immature fish, breaking the breeding cycle. There are no cutthroat in Tahoe today, but luckily the mackinaw confines itself to very deep water, seldom coming near the surface to feed. Today almost all Tahoe's shoreline trout are rainbow, some naturally spawned descendants of long-ago hatcheries, but a lot from periodic plantings. The occasional eastern brook and brown trout is caught, but they are extremely rare.

Fishing for mackinaw is not the sport of kings. Using heavy tackle, hooking and fighting a mackinaw that has struck a bait hundreds of feet below the surface is about as exciting as having a rock bump into your lure and then having to haul a load of wet laundry up from the depths. The fish does not fight and often comes to the surface with its air bladder protruding through its mouth like some gigantic bubble gum. They have a white, mushy flesh and are not even all that good to eat.

Fishing for shoreline rainbows, on the other hand, is as different as from night to day. Light tackle is used, they hit hard, they run, they jump, they often jump the hook. They are fun to fish for, and strike at lures either cast or trolled just below the surface. Their flesh is firm, uniformly pink and they are excellent on the table. So, we as a family, loved to fish for them.

One summer, now a half century past, Sarah and I took our two children, young Pete and Emily, then 9 and 7, there for a vacation. The weather had been beautiful, the lake glassy calm in the morning but sometimes kicking up in a wind in the afternoon, calming down after sunset.

But one afternoon thunderheads reared up above the mountains behind us, and we were treated to a couple of hours of rain, thunder and lightning with white caps on the waves on the lake. Then, as abruptly as it had started, the show stopped, the wind died down, and the sun came out. All that remained to show for what had gone on were good sized waves still washing ashore, but even they were calming down.

Very often that kind of weather leads to great fishing along the shore, perhaps because the minnow shoals have been dispersed and the trout go on the feed. After dinner we decided to see if this would be one of those times.

All four of us crowded into a little eight-foot Starcraft aluminum pram, and, with me rowing, set off south along the rocky shore. Emily and young Pete sat in the stern, each holding a rod I had rigged with a flatfish lure and let out line for a hundred feet or so. Emily's rod was my little 5½ foot Fenwick spinning rod I had built myself, and with which I caught trout, small stripers, silver salmon, even a bonito off the point of Cabo Frio in Brazil.

We passed familiar spots along that rocky shore, noting where we had hooked fish near this or that boulder, or hung our lures on shallow rocks below the surface. We passed the Sea Serpent, as we called a curved piece of driftwood with two knobs for eyes at one end jammed in between some boulders at the lake's edge. It did look like a sea serpent. We rowed another mile to Skunk Harbor Point and then turned to come back. The waves were still lumpy and rowing was not all that easy, but we made good headway. However, the trout were not cooperating — not so much as a tick or bump on either lure so far.

We were getting close to camp, just passing a rock taller than the rest, when Emily said, "This is what I would do if a fish bites, just like you told us to do!" and she pulled the rod into a bow — once, twice, and then three. At that point the rod stayed bowed — she had snagged the lure on a shallow rock, I was sure. "Here Em, give me the rod," and I started reeling in to pull us back to whatever rock was holding on to the lure.

But then the rock began to move. It was a fish, not a rock at all.

It fought doggedly beneath the surface, making several runs. Then it grudgingly gave ground, finally coming alongside the pram in the dim light of the sun, now down over the crest of the Sierra. It was indeed a dim light, but enough that I could see that it was a big fish, one set of treble hooks firmly in its jaw and the other hanging free. We had no landing net, so I decided to try to get it by the gills — or even hook myself in the hand with one of the trebles to make sure it would join us in the boat. I reached down, fortunately caught the gill and not the hooks, and swung the fish aboard. We looked at it in amazement. It was twice as big, maybe more than twice as big, as any trout I had ever caught in Tahoe or any place else for that matter.

We pulled in the other line and headed for camp, just a short distance away, took the fish up to neighbor campers who had a scale — 8 pounds 2 ounces, and 26 inches long. It would be almost twenty years before I caught a trout that large, and that one not from Tahoe. And fifty years later young Pete hooked, brought in, and released a brown trout in that part of Tahoe that measured 42 inches — indicating that it weighed well over 16 pounds. But Emily's trout stood out as a record for a long time.

The next night Sarah poached that trout in foil, white wine, dill and lemon slices. A dish fit for a king, no less.

Today we still call that rock where the fish struck Emily's Rock, so as to memorialize a truly great fish.

CHAPTER 4

ECUADOR

My work as a forester took me to Ecuador for four years during the 1980's. I had some wonderful times hunting and fishing there, the fishing limited almost entirely to rainbow trout.

Not long after I arrived I began hearing about a lake not far from where I lived in Quito, a lake where monstrous rainbows could be had. It was called Laguna Micacocha, or sometimes Antisana, for it lay beneath that big, craggy snow-covered volcano of that name out to the east of Quito.

La Mica lies inside a hacienda of a family that owned tens of thousands of acres in the highland páramo of the country, most of it above 10,000 feet above sea level and the lake itself at 13,000. Sheep were the mainstay of the hacienda's economy, though some barley was grown in the lower elevations. The owner, who lived in Quito and whom I never met, was a mercurial type and I was told you could never tell if he was going to give permission to fish the lake. If and when he did it was a written note to be presented at the hacienda's main gate. So if any opportunity arose to get there it should be grabbed at any cost. I was also told that the trip in, some 50 road miles from Quito, could be travelled in as little as four hours or as long as 13 or even more, depending on the season and road conditions.

The first time I had the chance to go was with a gang from the U.S. Embassy. We went in four vehicles, all 4x4's. Two were big Chevy Suburbans, one Isuzu Trooper, and then my venerable 1971 Land Rover. One Suburban and the Trooper had winches which, at the time, I thought were superfluous. Little did I know...

We assembled at about 7 am outside the Embassy and took off for the hacienda headquarters about 20 miles south and east of town, arriving in less than an hour. We rolled up to two gigantic wooden gates, closed and locked, with high adobe walls on either side. There was a hole in one gate next to the chain that secured it, and I could see a face peering out of it.

Someone got out of the first Suburban and presented a paper to the hole. A hand came out, took the paper, and withdrew. Moments later the chain rattled down and the gates opened to allow us through.

Behind the gates was a community of barns, corrals, and small houses out of the 19th century. We passed through and took off on a decent road, dry, well-graveled, but apparently with other bits and pieces of metal.

Within a mile I felt a drag on the steering wheel that could mean only one thing: a flattening tire. So everyone stopped while I changed the tire, which took a bit of time since we had to offload a bunch of cargo to get to the jack and lug wrench. Then on again, south and east against a northwesterly facing slope into which the road had been dug. We could see it snaking away ahead of us, ever downward and then a track wandering across at least a mile of flat, tundra-like land.

We dropped down, leaving the ridge and coming out into open land below us, dominated by the immensity of Vulcán Antisana a few miles to the east of us. That craggy peak, enveloped in snow and patches of blue ice, towered over us, a wisp of cloud drifting from its summit. It was a stark contrast to the dreary brown/green of everything else in sight, the surrounding hills completely barren of trees. We were definitely in the páramo, far above timber line, and the highest vegetation might have climbed 10 inches above ground level — maybe even less.

In fifteen minutes we had dropped down and were entering those flats, and here we ran out of the easy traveling.

Up to this point the entire trip had been in two wheel drive, but now the ground felt spongey, and all the vehicles went into 4 wheel. Without it we could not have crossed small gullies with steep sides that wandered over the marshy ground. First Jim Anders got across the worst gully with his Trooper; then I followed, too much right in his tracks, and spun out. Had I stayed only inches to either side of them I'd have made it, but I was ignorant of such things. One of the Suburbans tried a little to one side of me but with its much longer chassis it too got stuck; and then the second. Three out of four rigs immobile, and only Jim's Trooper on solid ground, the rest of us were going nowhere.

The Land Rover being the lightest of the three, we used a shovel to even out the slope of the gully in front of it, and using the winch on the Trooper, pulled me out. Then with more shovel work and both the winch on the Trooper, and its own winch, the first Suburban was eased out onto solid ground. With two winches the other Suburban came out easily and we had no more trouble across that swampy area and soon climbed to the top of a low saddle.

There below us at last lay La Mica in a broad bowl, two-and-a-half miles long east and west, and a half mile wide, with a steep ridge to the south. The descent was an anticlimax compared to the couple of hours we had just spent getting the cars out of that one gully.

We parked close to the north end of the lake on a flat bench, only a few feet above the water line, with plenty of room for vehicles and tents, so we set up camp there. Then the task of pulling out inflatable boats, pumping them up and mounting small outboards, by which time it was close to two in the afternoon. Rigged up our fishing tackle, and, boat after boat, set off clockwise around the lake. I had an eleven foot Sea Eagle with a 4-horse Evinrude.

The water was brown and murky, loaded with tiny invertebrate copepods, the mainstay of the trout's diet. There were no native fish in La Mica before it was stocked with trout, and I saw no evidence of any aquatic insects. The larger trout must have fed like baleen whales, swimming along with gaping mouths to suck in as many copepods as possible. Yet that diet produced large fish. Divers looking for a drowned man a couple of years before reported seeing fish at least five feet long at the bottom of the lake, and I heard more than one tale of a trout taking every foot of 15 pound test line and snapping it off when it reached the end. The strain of trout planted there may also have been responsible, since I had heard that they were Kamloops rainbow, which can reach 35 pounds or more in their home waters. Despite that diet they came willingly to lures, flatfish and spoons, instinctively attracted to them.

As the outboard puttered at trolling speed, our two rods bobbed to the wiggling of the Flatfish lures a hundred feet behind us. Ten minutes and Joe's rod tip bowed and he set the hook. His spinning reel sang and out behind us the water suddenly boiled. I cut the motor, and reeled in my line while Joe cranked to bring in his fish. It fought, making several runs, but he soon had it alongside. I scooped the net, and in it came, a nice three-pounder, the silver sides as if it were a fresh sea-run fish, though several hundred miles from any ocean. Whacked it on the head and slipped it into the cooler. We were not skunked.

We picked up four fish that afternoon ranging from Joe's three pounder up to about six. We quit as the wind started picking up and motored back to shore along with everyone else. The sun dropped and it got cold in a hurry, so we started a fire with the eucalyptus firewood we'd brought along. To get our food hot, though, we relied on propane stoves as well. At almost 13,000 feet, there was scarce oxygen to feed either, and it seemed to take forever to bring pre-cooked dishes up hot enough to eat. But with some bourbon, some rum, and some scotch, we managed to warm our innards while we waited. The campfire burned, but threw out precious little heat, and we were glad to have plenty of layers of clothing to keep us warm.

It was a motley mob around that campfire, the attorney general of Ecuador, the head of the country's inland fisheries, a trout fisheries consultant from Colorado, and four of us gringos: two from the Embassy and two of us from AID. We were a convivial group and had a good time trading hunting and fishing lies in both Spanish and English. By the time dinner was hot enough we were well-warmed internally, and food was an afterthought. We crawled into our tents and sleeping bags and I, for one, slept pretty darn soundly.

Dawn came all too early, and at five the soft chime of Joe's little alarm clock woke us both. We rolled out, partially dressed already, unzipped the fly of the tent, and stepped into a chilly half-light. The lake surface was flat calm except for myriad little dimples all over its surface — trout feeding on those tiny copepods. We did not bother trying to fire up a stove for coffee but stumbled down to the shore, the first ones up and out on the water.

While trolling with spinning rods was the accepted way of fishing, I had brought a fly rod with me to see if it could be possible to take a trout on a fly. I put on an olive-drab #8 woolly bugger with a lot of marabou to give it action, and we set out, the motor pleasingly starting on the first pull, and chuckling along at trolling speed.

First I let the fly line out about 30 feet, set the rod down and then started with the Flatfish on my spinning rig. It was about half way out when the fly rod started jumping up and down, threatening to leap over the side. I cut the motor, grabbed the rod and struck back. Line started to melt off the reel, but I managed to slow down the fish's run, and then started reeling back in. Five minutes later and there was the fish alongside, maybe two pounds, the woolly bugger well hooked into its jaw. By far the largest trout I had taken with a fly anywhere.

Fish in the box, we continued on around the lake, sunlight hitting on Antisana and its snows, but not yet on us. This time I let about sixty feet of line out on the fly rod, while Joe stayed with his Flatfish. Only a few minutes later and he had one on, this one well over five pounds, and a dogged fighter. Netted it and continued, me holding the fly rod now, and leaving the spinning rig in the boat.

It was not long before I felt a tick on the line, then a second tick and then a third. That time I struck back and it felt as if the fly had hit a wall — except the wall started moving off. The fish seemed unstoppable, but finally after running off line well into the backing it stopped and I started trying to recover the line I'd lost. It turned out a give-and-take battle, the trout pulling line out, my reeling it in, trout pulling it out, me pulling it in.

Joe started his video camera going as I slowly gained back the line, first the backing, then the fly line itself.

As I reeled in, the line went almost vertical in the water, and suddenly below me I could make out the shape of a monster trout wagging its head from side to side, and then with a flick of its tail, sounding again out of sight, the rod in an almost impossible bow, and the reel complaining as the line went back out. That big fish was at the end of a 7X tippet and not about to be intimidated.

"Joe," I gasped, "did you see that? You're going to have to try to net it for me when I get it up here next time!" He replied he was too busy with the camera, and that I had to do it. I kept the strain on the line, and slowly the big fish materialized again from the depths and came unwillingly to the side of the boat. I looked at my landing net and wondered how that trout could fit in that short, narrow bag. I made a swipe and in it came, seemingly two thirds outside of the net. I rapped it smartly on the noggin, took out the fly and sat back.

What a fish, the largest I was ever to catch on a fly. Later in Quito I weighed it — 7½ pounds.

The rest of the morning was an anticlimax. We caught three or four more fish and then came ashore to break camp and get ready to leave. It was then that I noticed that the Land Rover had yet another flat, and I had no extra spare. What to do? I had a can of Spare Tire, that compressed air and sealant, but the instructions said to run the wheel for five miles after inflating. Given the unknowns of getting back across that marshy ground a mile away, I decided to try an experiment. Put the transmission in two-wheel drive, jacked up the right rear wheel which had the flat, started the engine, put it in fourth gear, brought the rpm up to 2,000, and ran it until the odometer showed 5 miles as the Land Rover stayed in one place. Took it off the jack, packed all our gear, and headed out. Fortunately there were no problems where we had been stuck on the way in and we made the trip home without a hitch, the tire lasting all the way to the Pan American Highway. There it went soft but luckily a tire shop was right there to fix it.

One interesting sight on the way back was eight Andean condors dining on the remains of a sheep along the road. They waddled into flight as we went by, settling back in once we were past. What a magnificent bird in the air, its primary flight quills like fingers outstretched from the rest of the wings.

Thirty some years have passed since that fishing trip, but there are parts I can remember as vividly as if they had happened this morning.

La Mica is different now, having been dammed to provide more water for Quito, and who knows what may have happened to the fishery there. I'd love to go back, but that will not be.

TROUT FISHING EL CAJAS, AZUAY

In the province of Azuay, well to the south of Quito, lies a group of lakes called El Cajas, most all of them stocked with trout. I went there twice to fish, neither time with a lot of success, but both times were interesting. El Cajas has a reputation for being confusing since the landscape between lakes is tundra-like with scant tree cover. It is also subject to deep fogs and people have been lost there for days.

The first was a short afternoon fishing trip with César Galarza, an agronomist with the National Forestry Program in Azuay. We had worked together on a reforestation scheme being financed under the forestry project to which I was the principal advisor. In our off-duty conversations it turned out that we shared a passion for trout fishing, so he invited Sarah and me to come with him on a Saturday afternoon.

César was small, lean to the point of being skinny, but covered ground like a jack rabbit. Even with my long legs and being accustomed to the altitude, I found it no easy thing to keep up with him when we were working in the field.

We left Cuenca in our Land Rover about noon and climbed gradually, heading west. The day was clear, and we drove along the river that flows through Cuenca, draining many of the lakes to which we were headed. In a little over an hour César had us parked by the side of the road, we assembled our gear, and headed out a trail to the south. Sarah had her own little back pack with a book in case the fishing turned out less than red hot.

It took about twenty minutes over the narrow, twisting trail along a gulch to reach the lake César had in mind. Twenty-five years later I remember one steep stretch of rock face where only hand-holds kept one from falling into the gulch. The lake was not very large, perhaps a little over a half mile across. We set up and started casting small spinning lures, but the fish — if there were any — lacked interest. César said he was going around to the other side of the lake leaving me a space to work between us. Sarah meanwhile had lost all interest in casting, pulled out her book and told me to pick her up on the way back, as she settled into a little sunny lee spot behind a rock.

So I worked my way around the lake shore, casting, casting, changing lures, casting some more. Then, with no warning, the fog everyone had talked about was all around me. I decided that two hours was enough, and I'd head back to find S and we'd head for the car. I got to what had been a sunny little lee spot behind the rock, but no Sarah.

"Well," thinks I, "she's smarter than I and has gone back already." So I continued, picked up the trail, and twenty minutes later arrived at the road and the Land Rover.

No Sarah sitting inside. Panic. So I turned around and headed back, wondering what could have happened to her. Just as I reached the rock face a figure coming out of the fog — César. Sarah must be with him! But no, no Sarah. "Está Sarita contigo?" I called. "No, no está. Puede ser que ella se volviera a la carretera?" "No, she is not.

Could she have returned to the road?" he responded. I told him no, she was not at the car. "No podemos dejarla — we can't leave her" he answered, the understatement of the year for me.

And we took off again toward the lake. A hundred yards into the fog, and here comes a trudging figure — none other than Sarah. She had moved from the spot where I had left her, found a more comfortable one, and had gone to sleep. Why was I so bothered? There was nothing wrong. She was here, wasn't she? To this day we argue about it.

The second trip was longer and a little more productive, this time again with César but also a park guard who lived on down the same road another ten miles. Four of us, including two of César's brothers-in-law who had come from Cuenca leaving at 4 in the morning, and arriving not long after sunup.

Ecuador

Alejandro, the park guard, had five saddle horses and a pack mule waiting for us. As we assembled our gear, I had a two-man tent ready to bring, but César said his would hold six people comfortably, and we'd leave mine behind. So we did.

It was a long five-hour ride high into the south end of the Cajas lake region, especially for someone who had not been on horseback for years. We arrived to set up camp at a spot at least 12,000 feet up, not long before sundown. The camp site was in the lee of a very few stunted trees, the only kind growing at this altitude. César pitched his six-man tent, and I saw that it was going to be more than cozy with five, so decided to sleep outside. So I laid out my self-inflating pad and Hollofill sleeping bag. We ate a hastily prepared supper in the dark and hit the sack under a clear sky with stars and planets glaring at me through the black.

I crawled into my sleeping bag all but fully clothed with my insulated hunting hat firmly jammed onto my head. Then began one of the more uncomfortable nights of my life. A cold, cold wind, a freezing wind, was blowing as I went to sleep, my hands tucked inside the sleeping bag. But in my sleep I let them creep out to be treated to a blast of wind that seemed to be throwing slivers of ice at them. I woke up, pulled my hands back inside, got them warm, and fell asleep again. Out they came again, waking me up. Pull them in, thaw them, and go back to sleep. I don't know how many times that happened, but I found myself yearning for dawn, for hot coffee, for anything hot and edible.

And dawn did come and Alejandro got a fire going and coffee on the boil. I began to revive. It had been cold enough to put a skim of ice over shallow ponds holding trout, perhaps a quarter inch. Alejandro started fishing, using an old spinning rod with monofilament running through the guides, but no reel. Where he learned it, I do not know, but somehow he had developed his own brand of double haul, and he could put a fly out a good 20 feet. As he did, the fly would land on the clear ice, and trout would come from below, trying to break through it.

The day warmed, the ice disappeared and we fished. I caught a total of six but Alejandro did far better. I can't remember the fly; whatever it was it bore no resemblance to any aquatic or terrestrial we could see, but it worked. Nor can I remember how César and his in-laws did. But it was fun and an experience I treasure today.

By eleven o'clock we broke camp, packed up, saddled the horses and threw a diamond hitch on the mule and headed for home, five hours away. A longer ride I cannot recall, nor a sight more happily in view than Alejandro's guard cabin with his family outside. Packed the Land Rover, and headed back to Cuenca, the hotel, a hot shower and dinner. What a good time, but how stiff I was for days after that horseback ride!

FISHING THE ORIENTE

Every once in a while opportunity knocks. When it does, get to the door and answer. In the 1980's I spent four years in Ecuador as a forestry advisor. Since Ecuador's Park Service was part of the country's National Forestry Program, I had occasion to work with its people and to know several quite well. Flavio was one of them, an anthropologist who had studied in the U.S.

One day he said to me, "You like to fish, why don't you go down to the Oriente (the lowlands of the east side of the Cordillera, and headwaters of the Amazon) and go after the peacock bass and piraña. I can introduce you to people there." It sounded interesting, our son Pete was with us on a college break, so I said, "When could we go?" He told me to wait a couple of days and he'd let me know.

Sure enough two days later he came into my office and told me that it was all set up for two of us to spend a couple of nights with an Indian family out in the flooded area of the lowlands. All I had to do was get to Rio Oscuro by noon next Tuesday and we'd be picked up.

Ecuador

In those days Texaco ran the oil operations in that part of Ecuador. It ran a daily courier/passenger flight from Quito to Lago Agrio, (Sour or Bitter Lake, in Spanish) the main base for all the oil fields there, and usually had space to offer free flights to people attached to the U. S. Mission as I was.

So Pete and I pulled our gear together and one morning went out to the airport and climbed aboard. The flight was only about an hour or so, and we landed in Lago Agrio about 9:30, already hot and sticky. The town surrounding the neatly groomed Texaco compound was sleazy, a collection of ramshackle shops and shoddy vehicles. I asked around for a taxi, and finally found a yellow Datsun pickup available to take us the fifteen miles or so to our rendezvous point for a thousand sucres — about the same as $15. It was a tight fit in the cab, two good-sized gringos and a scrawny little Ecuadorian, but we managed.

The road was not paved but it was wide and graveled to handle oil well traffic, and in a half hour we arrived at a guard post for a pumping station, not far from where I had understood we were to meet someone.

So I asked how to get to Rio Oscuro, but all I got at first was a blank stare from the guard. Then he said, "Maybe it is down there about five miles. There is a cantina there with a billiard table." So off we went and sure enough, about at that distance we came upon a building.

The taxi driver went in to see if we were in the right place and even before he came out a good-sized young man in a baseball cap, wraparound dark glasses, a tee shirt and shorts came to the truck and asked if I were Arnold. How did he know, but yes, we were Arnold. So he went back in, collected a bunch of sacks and cartons, loaded them in the pickup and we drove down another mile to a bridge over a very small river, the very Rio Oscuro we were looking for. Offloaded everything, I paid off the taxi and told the guy to be right there at noon on Thursday, to which he agreed.

The dugout canoe we loaded was about 30 feet long, powered by a big Suzuki outboard. There were two native women already in it as we loaded up, and soon Luiz fired up the motor and down the tiny river we went. It was so narrow that it seemed impossible that we could negotiate some of its steep corners. The tree canopy overhead was so dense that we traveled in almost a twilight. We kept scaring up bats roosting on roots exposed on the banks, and they would flutter downstream ahead of us, looping up to roost again, only to have the canoe push them onward. We also flushed out several small ducks, close relatives to our North American wood duck, I am sure.

An hour down the little Rio Oscuro we joined a much larger stream, so wide that the forest canopy disappeared. Here the riverbanks were high, and there were native shacks here and there. At one bluff there was a much more substantial building, and the two ladies offloaded there with their supplies and we continued in the glaring sun.

Pete was still chewing Copenhagen snuff back then, and he pulled out the little can and stuffed a wad under his lip. Luiz wanted to know what it was, so Pete offered him a pinch, saying to me "Tell him not to swallow it!", which I did. Luiz tried it for a bit, found it wanting, and spit it overboard.

Another half hour and the high banks had disappeared. Suddenly Luiz made a left turn and entered a passage that was all but invisible. Again the canopy closed over us briefly, but then we were out on a vast body of open water with the occasional tree sticking up out of it. Before long we came to an island with skimpy trees and a small settlement of three or four native shelters. We nosed ashore and got out.

A large figure in a blue garment down to the ankles and a wooden crown was waiting on the shore. Figuring it was a lady I said cheerfully, "Buenas tardes, Señora!" to be greeted by a voice in basso profundo. It was the chief, not his wife. Luckily, he was more than a tolerant sort, or perhaps today my shrunken head would be hanging from his rafters.

Chief Carlos, father of Ray Ban glasses Luiz, was a dignified gentleman, totally native save that he did speak Spanish.

We unpacked everything and laid out the food Pete and I had brought, enough for everyone. Chief Carlos spotted the bacon and exclaimed delightedly, "Pura manteca! Pure fat!" So we were made welcome. They put us in the guest quarters that even had two raised platforms for beds, so we laid out our pads and sleeping bags on them.

By that time it was mid-afternoon, so it was decided we would wait until the next morning to fish. The rest of our time that day we spent talking about this and that, and I finally got around to asking how Luiz had known my name and was waiting for me. "Oh, we listen on the mission short wave every morning to news, local gossip and who is coming of going. Flavio posted that you would be there, and there you were."

We dined off mostly what we had brought along, but our hosts also offered smoked monkey, which Pete refused with ill-hidden horror while me, I just refused politely. And today, 28 years later we still don't know what smoked monkey tastes like. But we are not curious. We don't really need to know.

We spent an easy night, free of mosquitoes in the netting our hosts had provided over our pallets. Got up close to dawn and had a cup of the coffee we had brought along, and headed out for the fishing grounds in the canoe that had brought us here. Birds that looked like cormorants were roosting in the occasional tree as we went by. Chief Carlos told us they were no good to eat, but the eggs were tasty.

As we motored along Pete pulled out his snoose can and Luiz indicated to him that he should give some to his father, who accepted it happily. Unfortunately, no one told him not to swallow, which indeed he did. He spent the next half hour upchucking with me apologizing profusely. Pete's shrunken head deserved to be hung alongside mine.

Before long we began to see vee shaped waves in the still water around us. "Tucunari — peacock bass," Luiz said, "Cast out in front of one." So Pete unlimbered his light spinning rod and threw out a big Panther Martin as Luiz instructed, and the vee wave went ballistic as something headed for the lure, slamming into it and tail-walking away.

It was a good ten-minute fight before Pete brought it alongside, a five pound fish, black with the big orange false eye just forward of the tail. A real fighter.

Then I cast, but nothing chased it so I let the lure sink about ten feet before starting the retrieve. Immediately a tug and I had a fish on. We could hear it clearly as it grunted that far down in the water. "Piraña," Chief Carlos commented, and sure enough the noise was coming from the fish as it came to the surface. It was maybe 15 inches long but deep bodied like a perch, silvery but blood red about the gills and mouth, which bristled with triangular teeth. The chief reached down and with consummate care grasped it behind the gills. He was not about to put a finger where those jaws and teeth could snip it off.

We fished on, catching tucunari, piraña, another that looked very much like piraña but lacked the teeth, plus a couple of others I no longer remember the names of. But by the time the sun was well up the fish went off the bite, so our hosts decided to take us sight-seeing. First we went back to camp to leave the fish for the ladies to smoke, and then went on.

The open water stretched for miles, it seemed. We learned that nowhere was it more than fifteen feet deep, and that in the dry season it completely disappears, leaving a moonscape until vegetation rapidly sets in to cover the ground with green. The chief showed us where an oil spill from the oil operations had left a foot deep black smear on the tree trunks some feet above the water level. He said it had killed a lot of birds and other wildlife. It was an interesting tour, and we enjoyed it other than seeing the oil smears.

That evening we dined on fish, and there was enough left for our hosts to keep for themselves, which made us feel that maybe we were pulling our weight. After dinner they suggested we bathe, so in the twilight we waded out to about chest height, Pete and I somewhat fearfully, knowing there were piraña about and having heard horror tales of their feeding habits. "Unless you are bleeding," Luiz told me, "You don't have to worry." But worry we did, bleeding though we were not, and the water certainly was cool and refreshing and worth the dip. We slept well.

The next morning we did not have time to fish, for we had to be at the bridge so our pickup taxi could get us to the airport and the flight home. As a parting gift I gave the chief a Buck knife along with some cash I knew they could use. Since his son Luiz already had one from working in the oil fields, Chief Carlos seemed happy to have his own.

We made the long trip back without a stop, arriving an hour ahead of the noon time agreed upon. We offloaded our gear, bid Luiz farewell, and he headed down the river while we began to wait for our ride.

Noon came, but no taxi. One o'clock, two o'clock, no taxi, A bus rattled by but we did not try to stop it. Then we flagged down a truck to carry us to the guard station, so that when the taxi showed we'd have saved that much time. The truck driver dropped us there and we waited some more. Three o'clock, four o'clock, still no yellow taxi pickup and we had long since missed our flight.

Off to the west a gigantic black thunderhead was beginning to tower above us, moving east and threatening a thorough soaking if we could not find shelter. Nor was there room for the two us, our gear and the guard in his little telephone booth, either. So, finally I asked the guard, "Say, is there a gringo at that pumping station over there?" pointing to some buildings a mile or so away. "Ah sí, Señor Lloyd es el jefe ahí — oh yes, Mr. Lloyd is in charge there."

So I told Pete to stay there and I would hike over to see if we could get a roof over our heads that night. I got to the door of a building that looked like an office, stuck my nose in and there indeed was a gringo, talking on the telephone. He motioned me in, pointing to a seat as if he had been expecting me. He got off the phone and said "Well, what can I do for you?" as if I might be asking for the loan of a pencil.

I explained that we had come back from La Laguna to find that our taxi lift had failed us, that rain was coming, and could he provide us a shed roof to sleep under that night? We'd somehow hitch a ride to Lago Agrio the next morning. He said "Sure, we got guest quarters here you can sleep in, and the mess hall is open for dinner at six. Here are the keys to the pickup out there. Go get your son and your gear and I'll show where to go."

A little amazed by all this generosity, I drove the pickup to the guard station, collected Pete and baggage and returned to be shown to a room that Motel 6 would be proud of. Then Mr. Lloyd took us over to the mess hall for dinner, and a great dinner it was. He asked us about the fishing and all we had done, and then, "You were going to catch the Texaco plane at Lago Agrio? You don't have to go there. Our plane is going up in the morning and you can grab a ride on it." Saved! I asked how much I owed him and he waved it away. "Shucks, it's nothing. Just glad to be of help!"

So the next morning off we went on another plane and were back in Quito by ten. What a trip!

A month or so later Flavio, our go-between, told me there was a rumor that Chief Carlos and his entire family had been killed by narco traffickers. It was so saddening and it is so hard to believe that anyone like that could get to such a remote spot, far less have any reason to wipe out such good people. Two weeks later, however, as I went to visit the Chief of the Park Service in his office, who should be sitting in the waiting room but Chief Carlos, his wife and Luiz. It was like coming on

---

to a group of ghosts at first. I look back on how very happy I was to see them that day.

Then go forward two or three years. Son Pete and his college roommate were watching a documentary about Ecuador. Birds were roosting in a tree surrounded by water. Pete said, "They are no good to eat but their eggs are ok," and his roommate said "How do you know?" and then the voice of the narrator said exactly the same thing. Then there was a shot of Chief Carlos and his family, and Pete said "My dad and I stayed with them one time." "Yeah, sure" was the roommate's reply, so Pete pulled out his photo album and showed him a picture of him standing side by side with Chief Carlos. Proof positive.

So that was my one fishing trip in Ecuador where I was not after trout, and a most memorable one at that. Things have changed since then, and far for the worse. There have been more oil spills and more invasion of wells in their area.

TROUT OF LAGO DONOSO

I spent the years of 1983 to 1987 in the Republic of Ecuador as a forestry advisor to the U. S. Agency for International Development and Ecuador's National Forestry Program (PRONAF). For a long time I had heard tales about the fantastic trout fishing to be had in Lago Donoso, out west of the city of Imbabura, in the northernmost part of the country.

So, with forester Jorge Montesdeoca, my counterpart in PRONAF, we hatched a plan to do some work in the Province of Imbabura, and then sneak off and hike in to Donoso, spending two nights there enjoying some enviable fishing on a lake neither of us had ever seen.

We drove north from Quito on a Thursday morning, my saying nothing to USAID and Jorge saying nothing to PRONAF. We spent time discussing some AID-financed forestry work with the district forester of Imbabura and picked up some information about getting to Lago Donoso.

At noon we left, driving northwesterly to the headquarters of Hacienda El Hospital. This is a huge spread of many thousands of acres, the lake separated from the headquarters by some distance and accessible only on horseback from there.

As we were assembling backpacks of sleeping bags, fishing gear, food and cooking gear the local boss told us a pack train loaded with cheeses from a little settlement near the lake was coming in. It would be returning later in the afternoon and would take our gear. So we took off on the trail the locals pointed out to us, saying that it was maybe a four-hour hike. It was then 2 in the afternoon, so we should be at the little settlement near the lake there by dark.

The trail took us first up on a large rounded ridgeback well above tree line, and then across a broad tundra-like expanse of brown bunch grass, miles of it in rolling hills, the trail showing like a thread as far as we could see. About an hour in we met the pack train we had been told about headed toward the hacienda, and at close to five in the afternoon they overtook us homeward bound, our gear safe aboard. They told us we were only a couple of hours from our destination. That meant it would be dark by the time we arrived.

As we hiked, and as the sun dropped further and further into the west, with Jorge outwalking me by a good margin I told him, "I am slow, maybe because this is the first time I have been at 11,000 feet since returning from leave in California, or maybe because I just passed my 60th birthday, or maybe both. But I am slow." He laughed.

Onward we slogged, the sun went down over the horizon, and we were able to follow the trail by the light of all the brilliant stars overhead. Seven o'clock came, then 8, then 9. By then I was thinking we were going to spend the night, a cold night in the treeless páramo without even our sleeping bags, but we kept trudging. Then, about 9:30 we heard the distant sound of dogs barking as we came around a corner of a ridge dropping down to our left. As we dipped down into a little canyon the noise of dogs disappeared, and despair started to kick in.

We came around another corner to hear louder barking and see faint lights down in the valley in front of us. Heartened by that, we kicked up our pace, dropping down while the noise of the dogs grew louder and the lights became brighter. We passed through a gate and felt that by gum we were there.

Not quite. In the dark I managed to step into a narrow irrigation ditch not much wider than my boot was long, and as deep as my knee. In I went, pitching forward with a wrenching pain that caused me to yell. Why I didn't either dislocate or break the bones right where femur, tibia, and kneecap come together I'll never know, but they stayed intact. I pulled out of that killer ditch and hobbled the last quarter mile into the little settlement. By this time the dogs were going hysterical, but luckily they were all confined. Otherwise we'd have been dog burger.

Osvaldo, the man in charge, came out and guided us to a house where all our gear had been dumped, and with sighs of relief we pulled out sleeping bags and even found beds of a sort to lay them on. As I recall we managed to get a fire going and heat up some instant soup before collapsing.

The rest of the night was a torment for me and the knee, while Jorge snored tranquilly, oblivious to my woes. I had not brought even so much as an aspirin with me, and what I really needed was a handful of codeines. It was a pretty fitful night, one of those ones where you don't believe you are sleeping a wink, yet suddenly it is daylight.

We woke in a small settlement tucked away in a green valley with cattle pastures and a nice-looking river running right through the middle of the dozen or so houses on either side. Little rises dimpled the water. Small fish, but we wanted the big ones of Donoso.

After coffee and something to eat, Jorge and I put our rods together and, with one of the children of the settlement as a guide, set out for the lake. I was gimped up pretty badly, but if I had come all this way, I was damned if I was going to miss out on that fishing. Luckily it was an easy half mile to the south shore, and we made it in pretty short order.

A lot of lakes in the high country are edged with impenetrable, dense brush and small trees, making it all but impossible to fish from shore. Donoso is not, with easy access to little rocky outcrops along its banks. We put on Panther Martins I had made and started casting. Ten minutes and I had a good fish, a beautiful deep rainbow of a couple of pounds that fought doggedly but finally came in. Jorge knocked him on the noggin and laid him on the grass. And me without a camera.

And that was it. We fished until well after noon without another strike, and finally gave up. Jorge started a fire, gutted the fish, skewered it on a stick and did a great job of grilling it. A bit of salt and pepper we had brought along, and the three of us had a fine lunch.

Then the hobble back to the settlement, and a rest. In the evening we tried the river that ran through it, but the trout were all too small to hook. Where were the big ones? We never saw a one. We fished again the next morning with the same disappointing results.

Now came the realization that I was going to have to make the same long trip back, this time with a pretty unhappy knee. As we debated how we could tackle that task the boss man told us someone was headed back to headquarters on horseback and we could ride with him.

It turned out to be a couple of families that were going, the women afoot. They started ahead of us a little after noon, the women decked out in their gaily colored skirts and black hats. An hour later we followed after, with me sitting on a small horse and a saddle with stirrups far shorter than my long legs were used to. It was a trip of four hours, and one I feel to this day. But at least I was not having to hike it.

We arrived at Hospital before the sun went down, and I shall always remember how I slid off that horse's back, wondering if I'd ever be able to walk again. Turned out I could. While we were packing our gear into the Land Rover, the walking ladies we had passed on the way arrived at the hacienda, having made the trip only slightly more slowly than we. Talk about tough.

The drive back to Quito was long. I dropped Jorge home at ten that night and was in bed a half-hour later in the house on La Coruña. Not a very productive trip, but an interesting one. I could never do it again, but then I did not want to.

TROUT FISHING — RIO COSANGA

Down over the east side of the Cordillera that divides the waters flowing to the Pacific and to the Atlantic runs the Rio Cosanga, headed toward the Amazon. I had heard about the trout there not long after I arrived in Ecuador in 1983, and again a year later, when I met someone who had fished it. He told me it was accessible on horseback, so I asked one of the Peace Corps volunteers working down that way if he could rustle up some.

Then I heard from someone else that there was no horse trail, that you had to go on foot at the end of a spur road, cross one river and twenty minutes later find yourself on the banks of the Cosanga in its lower reaches. That source said the really good fishing, with big fish up to ten pounds, was a five hour walk up that river. Five hours to an Ecuadorian who does not wear a watch can be almost any period of time between the rising and the setting of the sun; also five hours at their customary trot eats up the miles something fierce, and beyond the powers of legs approaching the age of 60. So we decided to content ourselves with smaller fish down lower.

Sarah and I drove with Rumi, our three-month-old pup, over the top of the Cordillera and down the other side to Baeza, and stayed at the Hotel Nogal, the Walnut Tree, so named for a gigantic walnut tree growing above it, the largest I ever saw in Ecuador. The accommodations were rustic but comfortable and we spent a good night there.

This region was just moving into the dry season. In the wet season, from January to October some 27 feet of rainfall is common there. So the next morning we were not surprised to hear the first splats of large drops, one by one banging on the corrugated roof, followed by scattered pounding as the rain fell more heavily, followed by a steady, sullen drumming as it really got to work. But when we got outside it was only a "light" rain, nowhere near as bad as it had sounded, so we marshaled ourselves, a guide, and two Peace Corps volunteers, Ron Ziehn and Bill Schuette. We drove out some six miles on an easy road, ending just before we reached the first river.

The weather was still lowering and drizzly as we plunged into the darkness of the cloud forest, following a trail along the down plunging river. The trail quickly degenerated into a muddy track, crisscrossed with downed logs and pretty hard to get over. We reached the fording point, the river swift but shallow and the water clear, and sixty feet from bank to bank. No way was Rumi going to swim that, so Sarah put him in her little day pack, zipping up each side so that only his head was showing.

She took off with a staff I had cut for her, and Rumi stayed stock still, only the whites of his worried eyes moving — pretty rapidly. The rest of him was still as a rock.

We made the crossing okay, sat down, pulled off boots and socks, drained the boots and wrung out the socks, put them back on and released Rumi. Then on for another ¾ of an hour over another all-but-impassable trail, first climbing up one slope and then descending the other to find the Cosanga. The worst parts had been corduroyed with skinny logs. Rumi in short order changed from being a neat, fully furred black and white border collie with a white tipped plume of a tail, into a gray, muddy rat, but game as game. At times when he couldn't get over a log Sarah would pick him up and carry him for a bit, one large and one small gob of mud slogging along.

We reached Rio Cosanga at last, a beautiful river with a lot of wide gravel bars to walk on, runs, rapids, pools, and clear water running over cobble rocks of all sizes. By then the rain had quit and the sun came out, a gloriously warm sun among majestic clouds and patches of blue sky.

Now to fish. There were five of us, myself using flies and the others spinning gear. We worked upstream, casting into such fishy water that we had to catch something. Flies did not produce so I started casting a small spinner. It was just as unattractive to any trout. We worked the Cosanga for about three hours, finally giving up about 1 in the afternoon.

The others had picked up three or four little ones, 8 or 9 inches long, but Sarah and I goose-egged. And we faced the prospect of that grinder of a trail back to the road.

But the trip back we did in pretty good time, our walking staffs a big help in keeping up the momentum. And now we knew where we were going, which made a big difference. Half way back we found something that either we had missed or was not there when we passed — a gigantic dead earthworm, fully a foot and a half long and ¾ inch thick. Ah, for the trout to match that earthworm!

We forded the river, Rumi again in Sarah's pack, made the last couple of hundred yards and there in front of us our faithful Land Rover and a big lunch Sarah had packed. We sat there, eating and enjoying our beers. Then Ron, who stood about 6 foot 4 and had led the trek, looked at Sarah and delivered his highest accolade: "You are tough!" Indeed she was.

We drove back to Baeza to drop off the guides and Peace Corps guys and then made the long trip home, stopping at the Papallacta thermal baths for a relaxing hour in the hot water. What a great break in the trip

Excerpts from letters Pete wrote to brothers Tony and Stan while he was in Ecuador

To Stan, 7/17/85

It's shortly after 5 and in an hour we'll be taking Pete to the airport again, repeating the trip of yesterday. Last week he went into the Eastern office and said he wanted a reservation out on Tuesday. He was told that flight was booked up but Monday and Friday were open and which did he prefer? So he chose Monday. Yesterday morning at 6 a.m. a very sleepy desk guy finally realized that the ticket read Tuesday after all. So back this morning we come, ready to try again. Last time Pete's visa had expired and they wouldn't let him out of the country until it was renewed, which didn't cost anything. The reason for holding a person because visa has run out and then not charging anything to renew it escapes me.

Life in Ecuador flows on, sometimes smooth, sometimes bumpy. I've concluded that, except for a few people working in the office I am attached to, AID is stuffed with self-important bumblers who look like whiz kids of efficiency compared to the people in our embassy. Since neither S nor I are very social, and since we count so few of them as friends, we are not much in the American colony social whirl.

Enow, enow. I have spent the last two weeks trying to get all the formalities through the Ministry of Agriculture to buy six trucks with AID funds. The head of the National Forestry Program where I work narrowly missed snatching defeat out of the jaws of victory last week by a fairly spineless gesture, (author's note: what was the gesture — I can't remember. Odd, it was only 38 years ago) but I still have a slim chance getting them anyway.

The consequence of failing on this go around would likely be staggering, especially if we have to request bids a third time from U.S. suppliers.

I never thought that as a forester I'd turn into a purchasing agent.But then twenty years ago in Honduras I never thought I'd turn into a credit investigator of people with incomes of $100 per month when we were doing the housing study there.

I don't remember if I told you, but I have started tying flies again and even gave a talk in Spanish to members of my hunting and fishing club. For your information no dictionary here has the Spanish for half hitch, whip finish, tying hackle palmer style or woolly worm. I had to make up in enthusiasm what I lacked in vocabulary and I guess it went off well. I took a bunch of photos/slides of tying a woolly worm which turned out very nicely. Now I have them I should get on the Ecuador lecture circuit and perhaps do a version in Quechua for the native population. Their fishing gear of choice consists of Hercules hackle (dynamite), barbasco root that provides the toxic rotenone, and shovels. The last are used to block off small streams where trout go to spawn out of the lakes and strand them. One notch up on the sporting side, many are superb worm fishermen, I hear.

11/9/85

Hard to believe we've been here longer than we are going to be, leading to the wonderment of what we are going to do when we come home. One alternative which I casually mentioned to a U of Washington professor friend who is one of the Project's technical advisors, and to Phil Woolwine, is the possibility of teaching at its College of Forest

Resources, concentrating on international trade in forest products. They both are extremely enthused, perhaps more than I, and are busy beating the bushes up in Seattle for support from both the school and the forest industry. Who's to know?" (That one died an early death — the interest was not there, and maybe just as well. I don't know as I'd have been much of an educator.)

I was off on another fire — or series of fires — in southern Ecuador last week. At about 1 in the afternoon the Director asked me to go, along with the head of national parks, so we caught a commercial flight to Guayaquil, where we were met by a young army helicopter pilot, who guided us to his French-built Llama, a five-seater. I got the honor of sitting copilot, which gave me a great view.

We took off and flew southeast along the coast maybe 500 feet up, over what was left of mangrove swamps after a zillion acres were destroyed by a zillion Ecuadorians building shrimp-rearing farms. They are gigantic bare-ground patches surrounded by levees and fed by canals dug in from the ocean sometimes for miles. The only hitch in this multi-zillion dollar enterprise is that in destroying the mangrove swamps, it also destroyed the native shrimp breeding grounds. So there are precious few larvae to stock the ponds with. I figure that two thirds of the ponds we flew over were dry. And, ironically, we could see new ponds being built.

As we left the coast and flew inland the helicopter started gaining altitude so that we could get up to 10,000 feet and over the mountains to get to Loja, our destination. I was not paying particular attention until I looked down and then at the altimeter, which showed us at 5,000 feet.

In a sudden burst of panic my mind exploded with "What am I doing in this plastic bubble with a bunch of aluminum tubing and maybe frayed cable, built by a Frenchman and flown by an Ecuadorian pilot? Let me OUT!" The panic — most of it — passed as quickly as it had come, but I was left with a residual sense of unease if not malaise. I hark back to an Air France flight where I pulled out the plastic emergency ditching instructions, and its firm admonition: "Ne perdez pas votre sang-froid." (Don't lose your cool blood). Whoever wrote that had never been a mile above the Ecuadorian jungle in that airborne tricycle, or if he had he was being a bloody hypocrite mouthing such a platitude.

Actually, it was a good flight and an excellent young pilot at the controls. We arrived at Loja about an hour and a half after leaving Guayaquil, hot and humid, to step out into a cold and smoky late afternoon.

The next morning we left at 6 in the morning and 0 degrees C and once up to 13,000 feet, spent another 2 ½ hours overflying the fire area. At any one point there were no less than 15 smokes visible, each a hot fire burning really dry fuel but, luckily, in low ambient temperature.

Of all the fires visible only one was being fought, and that by a lone Peace Corps volunteer who had been a smoke jumper. I took gloomy satisfaction in remembering that when I was reviewing the project paper back in 1982 before I took on the job, I had noted the total lack of attention to the need for fire control and the need, in AID-ese, to "address the issue." This was a Park Avenue address indeed.

Luckily that night a cold, dank fog descended — so cold and so dank that it wiped out every fire, including one that threatened Loja's watershed. So our trip in which we were shuffling people, tools and equipment on paper, came to naught save for interesting times for me in the helicopter.

9/11/83

I'd put S on a plane and was batching it while she was in Albany

Since no alarums, excursions or anyone exiting hurriedly pursued by a bear having sounded I assume S arrived safely. I meanwhile went fishing this Saturday morning after a number of harsh words with Cholm (author's note: pronounced Chum, and short for Cholmondeley pronounced "Chumley," our 1971 Land Rover) who bitterly resents having to swallow Extra gas at $.30/gal, vastly preferring Super 92 at $.40. Unfortunately no Super 92 was to be had at our gas station, so he had to swallow the 80 octane. AT 6:15 in the morning he started to get even as my sidekick and I were about to take off. In fashion most tantalizing as I'd turn over the starter motor, Cholm would hiccup on one or even two cylinders and then fall silent. Bruce and I bodily pushed him backwards up our alley where he could start down the steep slope to Av. Coruña.

Compression brought him to life and off we went almost two hours delayed. Once warmed up I think Cholm could have run on bunker C fuel, but his awakening process is slow!

We went east over the top of the Cordillera on the road that everything must pass going to or coming from the oil fields in the Amazon Oriente — drilling equipment, well-casing, supplies etc going in, and lumbering trucks carrying oil coming out. Up near the top the road gets narrow, and it is a never-ending game of chicken as you and oncoming trucks close the distance between you. When I first started driving that road I used to pull to the right as far as I dared, given the precipice below. As far as the truck driver was concerned, that was a license for him to try to take up everything I had given up, the whole road, and so he would. So I learned to hold my ground to the last two yards and then pull over, squeaking past that big yellow frame.

Papallacta Lake lies just on the east side of the pass. It is maybe a half mile long and quarter wide. It was formed by a gigantic lava rock

---

slide filling the canyon, supposedly one of the aftermaths of a huge earthquake in about 1600. The road runs along the north side of the lake, and there is a pull out at the east end. Going around the rock slide end on foot is a scary matter, the boulders often unstable and covered with slippery moss. Trying to negotiate a passage with 59-year-old bones is fearsome. But we made an entire circuit of the lake without taking a fall, far less busting any bones.

I had 2 pound test line on my reel. It probably was older than I should have been using and I suffered the consequences. I tied a small Mepps spinner on and cast it out, hanging a really scrappy rainbow, all 10 inches of him. He left, with Mepps. I then lost four more spinners the same way without beaching a fish.

Bruce, who is not an experienced fisher, knew nothing of the concept of drag in a spinning reel, and it turned out that his was set at zero — no drag at all. As a result he hooked two fish that waltzed out to the middle of the lake, his reel screaming, and then spit out the lure each time. But at least he did get one beautiful 12-inch rainbow, deep, with a blue back, silver sides and only the trace of spots. And that was it for the day, and we quit.

It had turned rather nasty, cold with a spitting rain. With Cholm's radiator facing into the chill wind I feared for his attitude toward starting with all that plonk fluid in his tank. Sure enough, he showed utter and complete resistance to the idea of firing up. What down grade we had for trying to start by compression ran out without a hiccup of a cylinder's firing. We stood there helplessly wondering what to do.

About that time out of the mist comes another Land Rover, and the driver stopped to see if he could help. We started an impeccable conversation with very peccable Spanish on both sides until it turned out that he was a Brit, an Episcopal minister missionary. So he kindly gave us a tow until Cholm gave over and started running again.

After grateful thanks we started back up the 1600-foot climb to get over the 12,000 foot pass, Cholm duly furious at having been coerced into performing again. He missed, panted, hiccupped and almost quit at times the entire climb. Once over the top, however he seemed to give a shrug and say "Walp, win a few, lose a few," and took us all the way home that long downhill stretch without a burp.

Tomorrow morning he will go to the shop of Manuel and Pedro, Land Rover specialists, where he will undergo gastric lavage and maybe a high colonic irrigation to better adapt himself to plebian fuels. Can't really blame him since 80 octane is pretty cruddy stuff and he has run so beautifully ever since stepping off the boat six weeks ago.

Ecuador

HOOKED AT AN EARLY AGE. Pete with a striped bass at the age of about fourteen.

EMILY'S BIG TROUT. *The fish she caught at Lake Tahoe in 1968.*

HUNTING IN ECUADOR. Hunting doves and band-tailed pigeons in La Mica, Ecuador.

FIRST TROUT. Pete with first trout taken with a fly from lake Laguna la Mica in Ecuador.

Photographs

TRUSTY TRANSPORT. The Land Rover in Ecuador.

SAFE CROSSING. Sarah Arnold carrying our three-month-old pup, Rumi, while crossing the Rio Cosanga in Ecuador.

GETTING OLD. *Clicker in his later years.*

GADWALL IN THE BAG.
Clicker retrieving a gadwall.

ONE OF THE BEST. *Huck.*

HUNTING BROTHERS. *From left, Pete, Stan and Tony Arnold.*

START THEM YOUNG!
Dominic Barale, age 4.
Photo by David Barale

THE LAST TURKEY. *Pete and Tony with their birds on Tony's last turkey hunt in 2015.*

Photographs

CHAPTER 5

UPLAND GAME

DOVE HUNT

For us, dove season opened in the afternoon of the day before September 1, the official opening. Three of us, my son, JK (our host), and I, had ridden down in his UTV from the house to the lone scrubby black walnut tree along the fence line that sits on the south boundary of his 20 acres of mown safflower and wheat. It was my brother Tony's favorite dove spot where some of his ashes are scattered, and we had come to share a companionable beer with him.

There we sat in the shade of the tree, and watched the birds. We could have brought guns for there were a lot of Eurasian doves around, and there is no closed season on them. Instead we went unarmed, just for the pleasure of watching the flights. The shadow of the western ridge crept across the valley and up the slopes of the other side, the birds stopped flying, and we went back to the house.

At five the next morning we were up, had breakfast and sat for a while as dawn began to lighten behind the eastern ridge. A calm, cool time it was, and brought back memories of other dove shoots over the years. Then into the trucks and ten miles down the road to a friend's place along Cache Creek. It was still cool enough that my long-sleeved camo tee shirt was not quite enough to keep me as warm as I'd have liked, but not all that uncomfortable. JK had lent me his little 20 gauge auto since I had never shot one, and it felt nice and balanced in my hands. In the gathering light we walked out into a pig pasture, set our chairs and sat waiting for birds to come by. Only one did, which JK nailed. Otherwise the sky was blank for us, while shots were going off everywhere else.

The pig pasture had about thirty animals in it, ranging from 40-pound shoats to mature, 250-pound barrows ready for the butcher. All had ear tags, and none showed any fear of us whatsoever. In fact most of them were very curious about these two foreign bodies in their midst and some came up to almost within touching distance — but not quite. It was a little disconcerting that a couple of the larger ones were that inquisitive, since I could hark back to hearing as a small boy that every once in a while a pig's owner would become the pig's dinner, leaving nothing but boots and laces behind — maybe the belt buckle if the pig were not too hungry.

But then the pig's roach coach showed up in a pickup with breakfast in big plastic tubs the driver threw over the fence, restaurant slops and over-ripe vegetables and melons from the big organic truck farm, and we became non-persons of interest.

The flight, what there was of it, was over by 8, so we headed for home and breakfast.

TURKEYS

Well, turkey hunting got off to a rocky start last Sunday morning, when my son called me to the front door and pointed out a tom strutting his stuff at about forty yards alongside our driveway. Would have been a doable shot but for the fact that right behind the tom was the county road. Since shooting toward public roads is frowned upon, and since a vehicle can appear out of nowhere right in line, we decided that particular tom was safe and could enjoy Easter unmolested. About an hour later as I was taking in the sun and reading, I heard a commotion down the fence line, again about forty yards away. There was my tom on our side of the fence, and facing him on the other side a tom and two jakes, all four in a gigantic pissing match, pecking at each other. With a tight choke and a good aim there were times when I could have made a scotch quadruple, and all the time if I had shot at all, more than one bird would have gone down — and one bird is the daily limit. So I decided to let them all go.

Tuesday morning son Pete and I drove to the other side of the valley to be guests of JK, our traditional turkey-hunting host. By 1 we were all inside the tent blind, ready for action. But action was slow. First a couple of hens wandered by, one of them eyeing our blind with suspicion even though it was well brushed up. An hour went by, and JK noted some movement well upstream of us. Unable to keep his curiosity in check, he sneaked a hundred yards and came back. "Two otters playing on a mud slide," he whispered. Another half hour and a cock and a hen quail came past. The cock and I locked eyes, his vision partly blocked by his top knot getting in the way, but I got the impression that he had stripped the blind of all its protection and was staring at me naked. Then he seemed to shrug his shoulders and trotted off after his mate.

More of nothing until about 4:50 when JK decided we might do better fishing for bluegills and bass, so he went to get the truck while we eased our way out of the tent and walked to the road to meet him. We got into the truck at 4:59, and my son looked back to see three jakes feeding ten feet away from our blind. 5 pm and hunting day ended. But we had fun catching and releasing bluegills on little popper flies for the rest of the afternoon.

Next morning we went to a different spot JK had lined up. Turkeys had been roosting a little uphill of a vacant house belonging to a friend of his, and had been flying down to an open area in front of it. He had placed a couple of chairs for a blind behind a big bush to the east of the landing zone. We got there before dawn, walked the area, placed the dekes and I pulled on my face mask as we walked the thirty feet to the hide and settled.

As the dark started to fade, things became more distinct. Then turkey talk started. Then silence. JK nudged me and rolled his eye off to the east, a big bare field with a black blob in the center — a hen slowly, very slowly, making her way toward us, taking a peck of something, then stopping, then moving, the black blob getting larger.

But then on the other side of the bush I sensed movement. Slowly turning my head toward the maze of branches and twigs I suddenly saw at least a half dozen puffed-up males within twenty feet of me, strutting around each other. There was no way I could bring the gun to bear on them with all the branches in the way, so all I could do was sit and watch. Then a nudge from JK's foot — a strutting male behind him, providing a chance at last. Brought the gun up slowly, settled stock into shoulder, and lined up on the red head barely peeking above his shoulders. Blam! And down he went, not twenty feet away. I had nailed him in the head. A big jake, a tiny beard but seeming close to twenty pounds. So my turkey season was over before 7 in the morning.

I pulled off my face mask and in doing so checked to see if my hearing aids were still there. Nope, one missing. Looked all around where I'd been sitting, but no hearing aid. Showed my remaining one to son and JK, and in a half minute Pete reached down and picked up the missing one thirty feet away. Now that is the fourth time in twenty years that I have lost a hearing aid because of a face mask. Luckily three were found, and the fourth, forever lost, was covered by warranty. But wouldn't you think I'd have learned by now?

So that is the turkey story for 2018.

CHAPTER 6

MEMORIES OF THE RESPINI RANCH

It was a spring day in April, 1997, and I was driving alone though west Marin County on the Marshall–Petaluma Road. I don't recall why I happened to be in that part of the world, and I don't know why Sarah wasn't with me nor why I was alone. Maybe it was the month before my brother Stan died, and I wanted to get away from his sick room.

I came up the long grade from the old Magetti Ranch, and crested the divide between Tomales Bay to the west and the Walker Creek drainage to the east. There is a turnout on the top of the hill, put there for the gate that leads into the Respini Ranch property on the south side of the county road.

The Respini Ranch. From about 1953 until 1975 our uncle Roger Kent (Egbert, hereafter) leased the quail hunting rights on these 1500 acres from Philip Respini. In the two years prior to WWII he and a partner had leased the adjoining Magetti property but during the war Egbert went into the Navy and the partner failed to keep up the lease payments. When Egbert got back Magetti's was no longer available. By luck he was able to get the Respini property.

Philip was an Italian Swiss dairyman who had come over here many years before as a young man. His family and maybe others had pitched in to buy this dairy operation, sight unseen, and sent him to run it. Philip settled in, and then brought over a mail-order bride his family had chosen for him. To us she was always Mrs. Respini — no first name — always very quiet, always very welcoming. Philip died a long time ago but in 2012 Mrs. Respini was still alive at 95. Their son Dick and daughter Edith Rose now run the place, Dick's having changed the focus first from dairying to sheep raising, and then to a beef operation after coyotes made sheep raising all but impossible.

Egbert hunted the Respini place for some 20 years, accompanied more often than not by brother Stan and/or me, plus a varied assortment of relatives, friends and other hunting associates. As his hip and knee gave out from his hyperactivity in tennis and other sports of his younger years, in about 1970 he finally turned his rights over to four or five San Francisco friends he thought would use it well, and we younger relatives were out of luck.

Unfortunately Egbert's successors lacked the same drive to get over the hills after the birds the way we used to go at them, and their occasional visits lapsed into tailgate picnics complete with martinis, a few desultory shots at snipe in the bog, and then home. While snipe shooting they aroused a lot of ire from the Respini neighbor to the northwest, since shot would rattle down on his roof as a shooter would try to take a bird going over his head. They gave up their lease, and so, as far as I know, no one quail hunted the Respini property after they gave up in the early 80's.

I visited Dick a couple of times, and he told me that we were welcome to come quail hunting but (a) no snipe shooting and (b) we'd have to be careful with our dogs because there was so much poison coyote bait out to try to control their depredation on his sheep. None of us have wanted to take that risk, so as far as I know the place has gone unhunted ever since.

Now, years later, I pulled in and parked in the bright spring sunlight of mid-morning. Probably meadow larks were carrying on, and probably other birds as well, but these weathered ears don't pick up that pitch anymore, so the high hill was silent except for the noise of the gentle breeze out of the west.

I had stopped for a couple of reasons. One was the sight of small splashes of white dotted with yellow in the green along the road bank — blossoms of wild strawberries. I wanted to be sure that they were genuine and not some low-lying blackberries. And wild strawberries they were — a place to come back to in a month or so when they would be ripe. No fruit I can think of comes near the sweetness and intensity of flavor packed into such a small berry.

So that was one reason. The other was not quite as materialistic — the thought that probably Dick wouldn't mind if I trespassed a bit and hiked over to see all the places we used to hunt those years ago. So I climbed over the fence on the high, south side of the road, a combination of the old redwood pickets that used to march over the hill pastures of Marin, and the more modern field fence that should keep the sheep in and the coyotes out. The fit between pickets was narrow for my shoe, and I almost couldn't get it out as I made my way over the top and gracelessly plonked to the ground on the other side. Gee, it wasn't so long ago that I probably could and would have vaulted that fence.

I walked north, climbing gently up to the height of land. The grass, cropped so short by the Respini sheep, still had dew on it. This is hardscrabble grazing at best, and the droughty four years have made it doubly tough on the scant forage. The soils here are unforgiving black adobe, and it takes little to overgraze.

A blazing white puffball caught my eye. I pushed it with my foot hoping to find it still edible, but its interior exploded in a cloud of black spores that drifted away in a small cloud. No sliced puffball fried in butter tonight—far less any field mushrooms that dot these hills after the warm first rains of fall.

The top of the ridge was a scant hundred yards from the road, and when I reached it I could look down, down into the deep canyon, the last major tributary to Walker Creek before it turns into an estuary, an arm of Tomales Bay — Dead Horse Canyon we used to call it because Egbert and his son Keni had come upon one, in a state of magnificent putrefaction there toward the southwest corner of the property. There in front of me was the head of First Canyon — so named because it was always the first spot we hunted. It dropped north, straight away from me, north into Dead Horse. The tree cover, all bay or California laurel, the crown cover sculpted by the incessant west winds of summer, plugged the bottom of First Canyon.

Continuing around to the left, I began spotting other familiar places we had named in those earlier years — Dead Horse Canyon, Keni's Rock, where he shot his first quail at the age of 8? 9? — a fast bird zipping past him even faster since it was on a downhill pitch; and he took it with a .410. Skunk, where some dog (I can't remember who) made the Mistake; and Egbert's Perch, where he used to wait below the big rock at the last spot of First Canyon before the heavy brush took over. He'd sit on his British shooting stick and we ghillies and dogs would work up the canyon, flushing birds that would head downhill for that cover, and he would take them with his little Parker 28 with impressive regularity.

Across, on the high south side of Dead Horse, I could see where Stan, one time alone in a dense winter fog, realized he was Not Alone when first he was enveloped in the musky, uric acid smell of a billy goat. Then he saw, silently materializing a few yards away, the huge and majestic leader of the little band of feral goats that lived in that area. The fog closed back, and the band disappeared. He said it was one of the spookiest things he'd ever experienced.

But today was so different. While it was easy to see exactly where all those places were, something didn't fit. The light. That is what it was, the light. We were always there from late September through January, the hills only beginning to lose the brown of the dry summer. And here, today, in mid-late April, the sun was quite high, and everything was green — not only green, but light green, and even overexposed green.

During quail season, even as early as late September, the sun already is low, and precious little other than the wind-sculpted bay trees are green. And, as the season progresses, the sun gets lower, and while winter rains bring on the green grass, it is a different green. It is surprising how different the same place can look between seasons.

Egbert was ever the one for ritual, and our hunting routines were about as ordered as a Catholic mass. We would arrive at the Respinis' at about 9 in the morning, the Egbert car coming from Kentfield or Bolinas. First there was the greeting from Philip and Mrs. Respini, and some talk about weather and birds. Then we'd get out the old WWII jeep that Egbert had bought in southern California and Stan had driven up to Marin in 1946. Starting it was a chancy affair. Sometimes there was enough juice in the battery, sometimes not, in which case we'd hope that a bit of an incline would start it by compression. Finally with an unmuffled roar it would start — in fact I can't remember its ever not starting — and we'd pile aboard, three or four hunters and at least two dogs, Egbert at the wheel, and head for First Canyon.

That morning I looked down the brushy draw of First Canyon, lying there at my feet, and thought of all of us who had worked that climb back up the hill from where Egbert would park his jeep — his son Keni, brother Stan, Howdy, Terry, Fred, Larry, Bob, Lin, Lee, George — how many more? Of that list only five are still alive, and one of them drifting in the misty world of Alzheimer's. One was an editor, one a realtor, two were doctors, two lawyers, two foresters, one a rancher — a diverse group.

I started thinking about the dogs, the great, the good, the so-so, the magnificent and the worthless. The first that I hunted with over at Respinis' was Su, Egbert's black and white springer, who was always all business with nothing but quail on her mind. Then there was Loki, Bob Hunter's all-liver Springer-cocker cross he brought from the Islands and gave to Egbert, because she'd had heartworm and could not stay in that climate. Although she'd recovered, she had developed a nose-wrenching skin condition that made her less than a delight to live with — especially since she did crave affection. She also was all business, silent, humorless, but a terribly efficient machine. I remember going out with her on her first two hunts. On the first, she didn't know what we were looking for, or how to look. On the second, she was out of the jeep like a shot and working the most likely cover almost before we were ready. She stands out in my mind as probably the best Respini-land dog I ever shot over.

Tag, the magnificent Tag, Egbert's huge gentle golden retriever. On his way to being a field trial champion, Tag had wandered from the shining path and decided that some new retrieving events recently introduced he just didn't want to do. He was drummed out of the field trial circuit, and his owners sold him to Egbert — for how much I never knew. Not for a song, probably, but at far below the cost of his training. Tag was not usually a bush buster after sound and healthy quail, but I don't think any downed bird ever got away from him, even in the thickest of brush.

Clouds I and II, Stan's black labs. I just don't recall anything outstanding about either, except that I think Cloud I was the cause of Skunk's getting its name.

Speed, Stan's orange/yellow lab. Another silent, very business-like and thorough hunter. My partner Phil Woolwine once said of Speed, "If that dog were a human he'd be a CPA." No leaf went unturned if he was working a down bird or one that didn't want to get up. Speed ranked right up there with Loki in my book.

Osh, my black and white springer whose forebears were show dogs, not hunters. Mediocre would be the very pinnacle of words of praise for Osh. At best, he did hunt at the beginning of the day, and actually retrieved now and again. But get a jackrabbit's scent in front of him and off he'd go, yipping like a blithering idiot, never to come back until the rabbit had led him a couple of miles, I think. By midday, Osh would be happily trailing me in the brush, his nose on my heels, and not about to get out and do any work on his own — too tough and demanding. Osh was not a stand-out performer in the quail business.

Fred del Pino's lab mix, Sam, for Samantha, another Osh-type when it came to rabbits or deer. She was fast and relentless; a lot of del Pino vocal chords wore out along with mine out there in the Respini hills, and our voices probably still echo a bit through the remoter areas. Maybe the dogs' yips do too.

Flicka, our liver and white Springer, who learned to hunt out there once she overcame gun shyness. She was a good dog, not memorable, but eager to work and to please. It was such a delight, after Osh, to have a dog that didn't chase rabbits, and continued to work out front to the end of the day. Flick demonstrated one trait I've never seen in another dog; any time we had dead birds collected at one point, such as by the jeep, she would mount guard over them, and not let any of the other dogs within ten feet of them. She was that way with all dead things, even calves or lambs that died on our ranch.

If there had been recent rains we'd sometimes come across field mushrooms sprouting everywhere, and we'd first stop and collect bags full. Then on to First Canyon, down the slope where Egbert would park the jeep so that it still had a downslope for a compression start if needed. We'd pile out, he'd take his shooting stick to sit on as the rest of us and the dogs fanned across the canyon and worked our way up, pushing whatever quail might be there toward the top end of the brush. Once there they did not want to go higher into the short grass that takes over, so they would flush out, headed downhill where Egbert waited. But we too would have shots as long as he was not in the line of fire.

Speaking of line of fire, in all the years we hunted there I remember only one shooting accident, and that at First Canyon. Stan, Fred del Pino, and I were the beaters that day, and as we were working our way back down the canyon first one bird busted out from under Fred's feet, going past Egbert who swung on it. Then another got up and Fred fired at it, not realizing that Egbert was directly in line about 40 yards away. Egbert yelled at me to come over, that he'd been shot.

At first I thought he was joking because I could see him standing up, but then realized it was no joke. Got there and found a tiny thread of arterial blood spraying from a spot just on his left cheekbone. The tiny #8 shot had penetrated the skin enough to rupture an arteriole and cause the spray. He said that he'd felt the sting when it hit and then experienced a sort of optical illusion as a pink haze seemed to pulse in front of his left eye. I stuck my thumb down hard on the wound against his cheek bone, the shot still lodged there, and in a couple of minutes the pressure sealed off the arteriole and the mini hemorrhage ceased.

Stan and Fred (severely embarrassed) insisted that the hunt was over and we should get Egbert to the hospital immediately, while Egbert refused to consider it. I was suddenly the referee, Egbert's drawing on my Navy experience as a hospital corpsman to qualify me as the Senior Medical Officer present. I suggested that if the wound didn't open and start spraying again we could continue hunting. But if it did, then all bets were off and we'd head for home and appropriate care. Reluctant agreement by Stan and Fred, and we did stay the course and the wound never reopened.

That night Egbert went to Marin General to get the shot removed, and had to go through a mile of red tape because it was a gunshot wound. Later I recounted this tale to Lin French, our doctor friend who often hunted there. He said while he probably would have opted for the hospital immediately, maybe I had been right. So it ended ok.

First Canyon almost always took us to noon to hunt, and if so we would eat lunch there — sour French bread, Tiny Tots sardines in olive oil, and slices of red onion together with cans of beer, usually Miller's. Sometimes there would be a wild variation to this traditional fare if Egbert had hunted ducks the day before, in which case he'd bring the remains of the great steaks he would have barbecued at the duck club, thick, cold cuts of wonderful beef, always aged for 17 days before being cut up.

Then on to Split Canyon and Keni's Rock, and sometimes back to the ranch and down into the Walker Creek and Dead Horse Canyons. We hunted some damned steep slopes there, and I wonder today how my knees ever stood up to them. If I were to face them today those knees would say something like "If you want to go up there, go on. We are staying here."

As the season progressed and rains filled the bog below the ranch house, snipe would congregate there, and the day's start would shift to hunting them. There were a lot of snipe, and the shooting was brisk. Egbert would stand in one spot while the rest of us worked the bog, all his shots at birds flying overhead. Our shots would be at snipe getting up, usually in front of us, flying low and straight away at first, and then corkscrewing upwards in bewildering flight. If you didn't shoot in the first twenty yards of a bird's flight you stood almost no chance of hitting it. If a bird went down dead, it would disappear, fading into the ground and becoming invisible. We soon learned that you had to mark its fall with precision and not look away from it until you picked it up. We would never shoot at a second bird while going after a downed one. If you did, almost certainly you'd lose the mark on the first and maybe not find the second.

The day would end about three in the afternoon with the parking of the jeep in the barn and the transfer of guns, gear, and game to the car. Then Philip would invite us in to the warm kitchen to have coffee laced with grappa and a plate of Mrs. Respini's biscotti. Philip was a big man, balding with a craggy face dominated by a beaky nose, his English labored and strongly accented. But he would sit there and discuss problems with the dairy co-op he belonged to, or politics, or world affairs with a surprising understanding of what was going on. It was a fine and quiet way to end the hunt, and we would go home our separate ways with quail, snipe, and mushrooms.

CHAPTER 7

SEASONS OF THE YEAR

SPRING IN COLUSA

One day Terry Stephens and I came down off the foothills to pick up a friend who winters at the foot of the west side of the Sutter Buttes. Our idea was to come back south, pick up the Pass Road, follow it west to River Road and then north to Colusa for lunch.

As we hit the valley floor west of Marysville, someone had pulled the plug on the south end of District 10 — completely drained as far as we could see. I thought everything would still be flooded, but not so. All the swans gone from Woodruff Road, not even an ibis to be seen, far less ducks or geese. Crossed the Feather between Marysville and Yuba City, and it looked pretty tame what with their stopping the draw down on Lake Oroville.

But when we got to West Butte Road, just east of the Tisdale/Sutter bypass and turned north things changed. Water as far as one could see, walnut orchards 3 and 4 feet deep, and water running fast. Pass Road was closed, meaning that once we had picked up Pete we'd have to go all the way back to 20 to get to Colusa.

As we drove north, out in that vast café au lait sea we saw a good number of ducks, all divers — cans, bluies and ringnecks, from the look of them. They were in scattered singles and pairs, all swimming frantically against that strong current. They didn't seem to pay much attention to the red car as we drove by.

Picked up Pete, back down to 20 and lunch at Rocco's. As we headed back we decided to see what the River Road looked like. Crossed the bridge and the Sac and it was bulging, water as high as I had ever seen it. At the west end of the bridge a sign, "Road closed to through traffic." We hoped that meant the road north and the Moulton Weir, and turned south. After all, the ground out in front of us was dry.

Got to the Steelhead Lodge (now owned by Rocco's) and saw that if one were sitting on a bar stool inside he would have a very wet ass. Must have been at least 4 feet of water in the place.

Saw a pickup coming north on River Road and thought maybe we could get to Meridian and 20, and so continued until the road dropped off the levee to meet Pass Road — only to find both roads closed due to flooding. So, all the way back to Colusa and east on 20 to West Butte. This time as we went north the ducks nearer the road seemed to panic and flew off, leading us to wonder if maybe someone had instituted their own duck season. Same thing happened on the way back thirty minutes later.

So it was a long drive, this first day of March, but all the blossoms on almond and plum trees were saying "Hey guys, spring is here, it really is!" Walnut groves, still up to their asses in water, weren't so sure.

CHAPTER 8

SPECIAL DOGS

*O*nly those who have hunted over a gun dog will know the depth of the relationship that develops between them. And only those hunters will know the heart ripping grief of laying a gun dog to his or her rest after a lifetime, all too short, of faithful loyalty, hard work and undemanding selfless affection.

Of the many dogs Pete hunted with, and some are mentioned in Chapter six, two left their paw prints on his old heart more than most.

— Tom O'Connor

CLICKER

He was an auction pup donated by hunting and fishing guide Casey Stafford to the Gold Rush California Waterfowl crab dinner back in 2004. My wife Sarah and I, our son Peter and two very young granddaughters who loved crab were there, along with friends from Colusa.

When the auctioneer started the bidding on the pup, my younger granddaughter Ashley, who was six at the time and passionate about dogs, whispered to my son, "Buy him, Daddy, buy him!" But Daddy was not about to go out on that limb. Our Colusa friend Mariette, on the other hand, was. She dove into the bidding to the consternation of her husband, and came out the winner. Casey brought the pup to her, and she handed the black bundle to Ashley.

On the way home that night our son called his wife to tell her that one more was coming home than had left that evening. She was not impressed.

But when they came through the door, she took one look at the pup and said, "It's a good thing you're so cute or I wouldn't let you in the door." And because he had a little tab of white hair at the back of each paw, she named him Clicker, for the TV remote with white tabs for keys.

Despite the auspicious beginning, Clicker was not long for that house. He bothered the resident cats and a much older dog, and our daughter-in-law couldn't take it. Our son called and told us Clicker would have to find a new home. "That's all right," I quickly said. "We'll take him." And take him we did.

In his early life he was a CWA dog, first going with me as a pup when I volunteered to help in the CWA kids' booth at the International Sportsman's Expo, where he and the kids had wonderful times together as they played with him and watched him retrieve. Then after trainer Bethanie McGahan did a great job of teaching him, we went to CWA field days at Conaway Ranch and Rancho Esquon, where she'd show the audience how retrievers worked. I like to think she considered him one of the best dogs she'd ever trained. In years after I had to give up volunteering, CWA staffers involved in those activities used to ask after him.

Clicker had the makings of a great field trial dog, but as anyone who so generously hosted us on duck hunts will remember, he was all but intolerable as a blind mate. If there was no action, he whined, he moaned, he couldn't stay still.

In later years, when I had to give up hunting public grounds, my son would take him out. More than once Clicker made such a fuss that Pete quit after only an hour and took him home. There was no way I could find to cure him of that dismal behavior. Roque Merlo, who owned his sire, told me later that one of Clicker's litter mates had the same problem and never got over it. Hereditary, perhaps?

But if there was action, Clicker was all business, and when a bird fell he was flat out after it. As fast as he went going out, he was just as fast coming back, every time. I've watched other dogs go out fast, but once the bird was in hand, come back at a much more leisurely pace. Not Clicker. For him it was high gear all the way.

I'll always remember the first bird that dove on him, and how quickly he stuck his head underwater to grab it as if it was something he had always done.

REFLECTIONS FROM CLICKER'S TRAINER

Clicker was so fun to train because of his "Ah ha!" moments. If he struggled and then got the concept, he would be so excited. Then he would retain the concept and it became an easy generalization for the next lesson.

His attention to retrieving was so natural. He was very personable and happy with his "people." He would light up when he saw you, and it was neat because even if I wasn't feeling good about myself before a training session with Clicker, I felt like the best dog trainer in the whole universe by the time it was over.

I really loved those days and Clicker. Thank you for all the fun and sharing your dog with us!

— Bethanie McGahan

MY MEMORIES OF CLICKER

He was perhaps the most genial dog we ever had. He had not a mean bone in his body, was truly a people dog, and loved everyone, including dogs, but not cats. Cats he just ignored. And when he was home he turned off his hunting button. One time he was lying in the sun and several wild turkeys sauntered in. He just lifted his head at the sound of them walking by and went back to sleep.

As I aged and had to give up on going out to the wildlife areas, he got cheated out of a lot of hunting while he was just passing his prime of life. While my son took him occasionally, he should have gotten a lot more time in the field than he did. He became pretty much a house and yard dog.

And then age started catching up with Clicker too. The hairs around his nose and mouth started to grizzle, and he began a general slowing down. Eventually infirmities started crowding in on him, a touch of dementia, deafness, increasing weakness in his hind quarters, weight loss, strained breathing as summer heat came on, fading vision.

Life was not happy for him, so we made that excruciatingly painful decision.

This morning, 14 years after that fateful crab feed, the vet came, and Clicker went from us amid our tears to the Great Marsh in the Sky where ducks keep falling for him to retrieve.

I so hope it was a blessed relief for him. Farewell, Clicker. May we meet again when I cross the Great Divide. You were a wonderful friend and are dearly missed.

Thank you, CWA, Casey Stafford, Mariette, and Bethanie for 14 happy years with such a great friend.

HUCK

How does someone pick a dog for a hunting companion? I have heard many tales of people's searching out which breed they should select, then searching blood lines to narrow the field, then carefully looking over litters of those blood lines to pick out the ideal pup, testing him/her with bird wings, for level of aggressiveness, or any other thing that might make a difference. And, after sifting out that way, and finally picking out the perfect dog, not all that seldom those self-styled perfectionists wind up with a hunting dud — maybe a great family dog, but no one to share the duck blind with.

In the case of Huck, my main criterion was, I wanted a German Wire Hair. I was not particular as to its origin or blood lines, I just wanted the same breed as old Yank, my friend Rod Williams's whiskered, solid liver GWP, in whose company I had hunted ducks, geese, quail and pheasants for a number of years.

One day I picked up the classifieds of the Sac Bee and found an ad for GWP pups, with a South Lake Tahoe phone prefix. Since I was headed that direction for a meeting anyway, I called and made an appointment to look at what was available.

On arrival the lady of the house ushered me into a screen porch, and the three pups remaining from the original eleven (some kept alive by mouth to mouth resuscitation at birth, she told me) were brought out for my inspection. Two were males, and sported no whiskers or bristly coats. The third, much smaller, was a fully clothed female. I set my sights on her, only to be told that she was not available, the owners were going to keep her. So I was left with two alternatives.

By that time the pups were four months old, more than twice the ideal age for going to new homes. And the two males were BIG, already well over a foot high at the shoulder, larger than a mature fox terrier.

One of the males promptly lay down and went to sleep. The other came over to me, sat down next to my knee, leaning against it, and looking outward, started gently chewing on a brochure I held in my hand. So much for testing the pup for birdiness, for alertness, for responsiveness. I was hooked, so home he came.

(A footnote: two years later I ran across the owner of Huck's parents and his sister whom I had wanted. I asked how she had turned out. "Terrible," he told me, "she doesn't like to hunt, but we love her.")

The kids in the family where he was born had called him Scooby Dooby, a name I didn't like much at all. Anyone working with dogs knows that to get a dog's attention its name should be short, never more than two syllables, and preferably one. For some reason I cannot remember, I had decided to call him Dandy. He held that name for a few hours on our trip home, but shucked it off as soon as our daughter saw him. "His name," she stated in no uncertain terms, "is Huckleberry Hound." Well, from two syllables to five sort of trashes the idea of a short name, but since it could be cut back to just Huck, it seemed like a good choice. "Dandy" disappeared in a flash, and Huck he became. Looking back on it, there could have been no other more appropriate.

In later years in the field there were embellishments, depending on how independently Huck was hunting. Robin Blackmore, a New Zealand hunting guest, tagged him with "Goddammit Huck," why I have no idea, except that the name followed a day of Robin's hunting with us, and of Huck's apparent total hearing loss when I was admonishing (aka yelling) at him.

I'll not forget the sense of despair that I felt the first time I wadded up a piece of paper and tossed it out in front of this new pup. Instead of tearing after it, pouncing, and bringing it back to me, Huck looked first at it, and then at me with an air of total puzzlement. "What did you do that for?" he seemed to be trying to say. It held no interest for him whatsoever. Had I chosen a dud?

But then a couple of days later I bought one of those rubber boat fender retrieving dummies. The first time I tossed it out he was on it in a flash, bringing it back proudly. My despair had been groundless. From then on he would retrieve anything I threw.

He took very quickly to the training, such basics as sit, come, stay, and responding to the whistle. I never went beyond those kindergarten steps of training, the fine points of marking and holding when I threw dummies, or getting him to respond to "Whoa" if he was running too wild. Later I used an electronic collar for that purpose, just enough juice so that he would remember that he wasn't the only one out there. He'd get out too far, I'd nick him, and he'd act as if he had just thought it might be a good idea if he came back toward me to make sure I was still with him.

While he didn't mind water, he was not gungho about diving in, often taking an almost lady-like approach to getting himself wet before striking out after the dummy. I wondered a bit about what would happen out in the duck blind if he was going to be so deliberate. He turned out to be a really fine water dog. His height made it unnecessary for him to swim in depths where a lot of labs could not stand, giving him a major advantage in being able to gallop instead or having to swim after downed birds. When we hunted the tule ponds of the public hunting grounds he'd stand silent and still by my side, never moving unless he saw a bird come down. Then he'd take off, and it was very seldom that he would return empty mouthed.

Huck had a huge vocabulary, but we never got to the point of my understanding most of what he was saying. Any time someone came to visit Huck would greet the guest with all kinds of long drawn out talk, probably asking where they had come from, had it been an easy trip, and how glad we all were to see them.

And if I were to pull out hunting gear, it was Katie bar the door. I'd get an earful about the good time we were going to have, where were we going, who were we going with and what were we after?

He had an inventory of groans, barks, and long drawn out "A-ou-ou-ou"s when happy to see someone. We knew that he was really going downhill when he stopped vocalizing completely the week before we had to face the grim task ahead. Up to then he had a special routine if he thought dinner was late in being put before him. He'd come nudge me first, and if I did not respond, he'd start mumbling with his mouth closed and nudge me again. If this didn't work he'd open his mouth and start nipping my elbow while grumbling in the back of his throat. That would usually work, and if I got up then he would head happily for the door, all the time going "Ooh-Ooh-Ooh!"

You could also get a rise out of him just by asking what he wanted. He'd cock his head to one side bring his ears forward, and say a number of incomprehensible things that were probably not very nice.

He was extremely sensitive to the sound of sirens, and would respond with long, drawn out howls that would last for a minute or two. Often they were far enough away that I couldn't even hear the sirens he was answering.

For the first five years of his life Huck seemed to live to play. Any dog he met in those years was a built-in playmate, whether the other dog knew it or not. Lots of times the other dog would not respond the way he wanted, but that didn't seem to faze Huck. The new friend was a playmate whether he wanted to be or not.

For a couple of years we also had a little black Schipperke, whose whole body was not much larger than Huck's head. They had a game of tag where Huck would chase Skipper around the car on the parking pad. If it looked as if Huck was going to catch up, Skip would nip under the car where Huck could not possibly go.

Senior moments cloud my memory of where I first took Huck hunting, or what we were after. I think it was planted pheasant and chukar at Yankee Slough. I had already checked him for gunshot tolerance by taking him to the local trap range, initially leaving him in the car and eventually out to behind the firing line. He never flicked an ear to the gunfire around him, nor ever after.

He had his first opportunity to hunt when a friend and I bought season's memberships in the Glenn Pheasant Club, giving us rights to hunt on various pieces of private property near the town of Glenn on the Sacramento River. They weren't very productive properties, and I don't think either of us got more than a couple of birds the whole season.

Opening day of pheasant season is the same as opening day of the late dove season, but we saw no doves on the property we were hunting, At 8 months Huck was not really in his element, but he was working a ditch line and thinking he was being birdy. Suddenly he locked into a point, and I tensed up waiting for a big rooster to flush out. Nothing, I urged Huck in and he moved a foot. Nothing. Urged him again. This time his head darted out and up he came with a wing-tipped meadow lark. Someone hunting before we got there must have shot it thinking it was a dove. Huck turned to me, I put my hand out, he dropped the bird and immediately it fluttered off. He dove, picked it up and delivered again. Again I failed to grab it and fluttered away. I think this happened five times before I finally got my hand around it, and, save for a bit of slobber it was unharmed except for the wing. I had a soft-mouthed dog!

Huck turned into a very meat and potatoes kind of hunting dog, good both on upland game and on waterfowl. His pointing style left a little to be desired in my opinion. One likes to think of a dog standing rigid, tail up, one foot raised. When Huck came upon a bird he would first freeze, and then flatten himself on the ground. If the bird moved he would waddle after it, still flat down there. Then it would flush, and he would break to chase it. Not good manners at all. But he was also tenacious. One time, pheasant hunting with Robin Blackmore, Huck started nosing about a batch of berry bramble maybe ten feet across.

He'd push in from one side and then have to back off from the thorns to try another entry. He could not penetrate into the middle, but he kept at it for probably ten minutes. I was ready to call him off when a rooster exploded out of the center, climbing fast. I shot twice at it, missed, Robin shot twice at it, and missed. A moment later I heard his voice, very low: "If you don't tell anyone, neither will I." Well Robin, twenty years later the truth is out.

After waterfowl, Huck would sit by my side or by the blind, rock still for hours at a time. But when a duck or goose went down he always had a perfect mark on it. He did not lose birds. In fact, more than once if we were wading to a distant blind he would disappear, and a few moments later I would sense him at my side, looking up at me with an almost apologetic expression, a crippled duck in his mouth. He seemed to me to be saying "I know you didn't shoot this, but would you like it?"

Eleven years went by all too very quickly, and like many larger build dogs Huck suddenly began to fade. He had been bitten in the right rear foot by a big rattlesnake and survived it, still with a limp. But then he developed a tumor on his left front wrist. The vet mentioned the possibility of amputating that leg at the shoulder, but that would have all but immobilized him. We had to make that awful decision and one summer afternoon the vet came and we said good bye to a most remarkable friend. We shall always miss you, dear dog.

TOM'S MEMORIES OF HUCK

While the guest of the CWA Hunter Exchange Programme with New Zealand in 2001 I spent a few days hunting with Pete and his German Wirehaired Pointer Huck. On a clear day we went out after pheasant and snipe but Pete forgot to take the all-important control collar and

Huck's enthusiasm knew no bounds. We bagged a snipe or two and a big Canada honker that was foolish enough to drift over us but Huck managed to flush a good many birds way too far ahead of us for a shot. Pete's growing frustration coupled with Huck's unashamed and boundless energy made it one of the most memorable days of a truly memorable and all too short stay in California. That dog had such a wonderful personality that it was impossible to even chide him on his return. He had a great day even if we didn't and who could deny him that. On my return to New Zealand I wrote this tribute to Huck and Pete, and I have fond memories of both of them.

— *Tom O'Connor*

A COUPLET FOR A GOOD DOG

A handsome hound was Huck, with full long leg and deep of chest,
When game was up and birds were a-wing he'd sit by the kitchen door,
He'd hunt all day and half the night and wag his stump for more.
A twinkling eye above, a wet smile below ~and a busy nose of the best.

So they went a-hunting then; his master and another, among the
    marshes strode,
Huck to the fore, guns behind they sought snipe, pheasant duck and
    drake
With blood full up, and legs full stretch, Huck left the guns a-struggle in
    his wake
Even tho' he took the rough tracks and game trails; the hunters walked
    the easy road.

Crashing through the rushes, plashing through the muddy creeks,
But far behind and full a-flounder the guns could not match the pace,
So Huck had the field to himself and was set to win the race.
Here were birds a plenty on the jump, if only the guns would speak.

Special Dogs

"Call him in, slow the charge," they needed time to breathe,
For Huck was a free agent this day with naught to halt his fun,
With all the world before him and miles and miles to run.
But no whistle was at hand, and their rage began to seethe.

He hunted high, he hunted low, he hunted far away,
Master's voice thin and reedy grew. Anger was all boil and simmer,
Of obedience and discipline there was not the slightest glimmer.
And how the birds did flush most willing, he had a wondrous day.

I like you Huck, you scoundrel; your free running spirit of ease
Nor any sign of guilt or remorse cross your happy face that day,
Brace after brace of pheasants you flushed and chased them far away
With none to rein you in, you ran as far as you pleased.

If only I were like you with speed and skill and none to hold me back
I could follow my dreams as far as my courage, will let me
Take the risks, play the long ones and see what there was to see,
If I only had your heart to hunt at my own pace along life's marshy
      scented track.

— Tom O'Connor

CHAPTER 9

LAST HUNT

In the dark he heard the dog's tail thump, and he reached for the light switch. His internal alarm clock had already alerted him, and the tail thump confirmed it was time to get up. Sunday morning, last day of the duck season, and he and his dog were the only occupants of the old club house. This morning he would be drinking coffee alone in the kitchen, quite a change from yesterday when, exactly an hour before shooting time, seven other members besides himself had crowded around the photo map of the marsh on the kitchen wall to make their choices according to the draw for that day.

A ladder of names that hung next to the map contained each member's name neatly lettered on a wooden rung. All through the season, every shooting day the position of names showed members in their order of priority of choice for that day. On the big photo each blind location was marked by a cup hook screwed into the map, and as the hunters made their choices, tags with their names went on to the hooks. It was a tradition still carried on for close to a century, the only difference from back then and now was that in the old days it had been a pen and ink map show and now was an enlarged print of an aerial photo.

This morning showed how yesterday's No. 1 choice had gone to last place, and No. 2 was now first, while his was right in the middle. Of course it didn't matter, since all the other hunters had left after the previous day's shoot, but it was, after all, tradition, and, in old duck clubs, traditions are to be observed. His choice was going to be first, last, and only this morning, no matter where his name appeared on the ladder, but he would not place his name tag on the wall until exactly one hour before shooting time.

He made his way down the long, tilted, narrow hall toward the kitchen, the members' small bedrooms on either side. The hall was so narrow that there was no room for conventional hinged doors, so pocket doors slid back into the walls, each with its own characteristic rumble. The dog's tail beat a tattoo against them as she trotted behind him. When other members were there it acted as an alarm clock for them.

Into the dark paneled living room with its wide fireplace, poker and domino table, big comfortable couch and chairs, under the big mounted Canada on set wings over his head, past the long dining table, through the crooked doorway and into the kitchen with its canted floor. Let the dog outside to drain, turned on the coffee maker, waited for the dog to come back after doing her business. Then back to his room to get dressed while the coffee maker burped and hiccupped to itself.

Suited up in his chest waders, jacket, gun and cartridge bag in hand, duck and goose calls in the lanyard about his neck, he returned for a cup of coffee and a stale pastry from yesterday's breakfast. He sat there in the harsh glare of the fluorescent tubes in the ceiling, looking at the wall map and trying to decide which of the dozen blinds he should choose. It was clear outside, and no wind to speak of, so the choices were many and probably few really promising.

He finally decided on Blind No. 9. Shooting time this last day was at 6:45, so as 5:45 arrived, he ceremoniously took his name tag and hung it on 9. By now the dog was getting antsy. Sitting next to him she insistently nudged her black head under his elbow. "Come *on*! Time to *go*! The birds will all be *gone*!" So he finished his coffee, put the cup in the sink, turned out the lights and stepped outside into the dark.

The gravel crunched under his feet as he looked at the sickle waning moon in the clear eastern sky, climbing above the far Sierra. Stars glittered out of the blackness. Off to the west were the lights of the housing developments along the new freeway. Not too many years ago it would have been blank dark over there, but not now, thousands lived where once it had all been dry pasture, with car and truck traffic where before it had been silence. The subdued roar of vehicles now all but drowned the natural noises of the marsh.

He opened the rear hatch door of the car, stowed his gear, told the dog to kennel up, closed it, got into the driver's seat and started the engine. Two miles to go. Up onto the levee, past the line of eucalyptus trees that were home to egrets and night herons, and on past the impenetrable walls of blackberry on either side, watchful for skunks that might be shuffling their way home from a night of foraging. Not good to bring a smelly car back to his wife.

Then, past the blackberries, the marsh pond opened up on his right. The headlights picked up the flicker of wings as ducks jumped from the edge of the grass and water. New birds in, he wondered? Not likely this late in the season.

On along the narrow track until the white post with the number 9 appeared in the headlights' beam. He pulled the car over into an area so others could get past, even though no one else was going to be here today. Opened the door and, stiffly with the waders hampering, eased out, went around to the back and opened the rear door to let the dog out and get his gear.

A pack for shells and water, a sack with his 8 good luck widgeon decoys, his gun in a leather scabbard, and a ski pole, and he made his way to the water, the black, black and stinky shallow water that never gets a chance to circulate the way the deeper water does. The reflections of stars winked at him between the pickle weed as he waded out, barely ankle deep.

It was a long 200 yards out to the blind, the water getting to shin deep, the dog galloping ahead, checking for fresh duck smells, and finally finding her spot next to the blind. He got there, pulled one lid off, and laid down his gear. Then the sack of widgeon dekes to put out among the rest of the decoys already there. Did those eight birds make a difference in attracting passers-by? Probably not, but, like putting the tag on the cup hook, it was tradition with him.

Now the tedious job of shoehorning himself into the barrel blind. One foot reached down, found the stool on the floor, and he put weight on it. Laboriously he pulled the other booted foot into to blind, searched, and it too found the stool. Resting his elbows on the rim of the blind, he moved the first and then the second foot to the floor, and he was in. Too cold for black widows to be active this morning so he did not have to check for them. He had very bad feelings about spiders, especially black widows, though none had ever bitten him.

He pulled the gun out of the scabbard. It was an old gun, a double barrel 12 gauge Greener his father had left to him, and he treasured it as an old friend. Then he laid the scabbard on a hook, and then his pack. Broke the action on the Greener, reached into the bag, pulled out two shells and loaded them into the barrels. No steel shot for this gun, it needed far more expensive nontoxic shot, but he was willing to pay the price. Now he was ready.

Some lessening of the dark off to the east; dawn was on its way. To the west where the marsh met the high ground, the muted roar of traffic even at this early hour. He thought back to his boyhood days when the only sounds of man on the marsh were those of the freight trains pounding past the club, the giant cab-in-front Mallet steam engines making the marsh quiver as they thundered along the rails. They went by several times a day. By contrast, only once a day in the early morning would pass the yellow and brown diesel-electric streamliner passenger train, City of San Francisco, bound to Oakland from Chicago. It would drift past, swiftly and eerily silent compared to the freights.

And what had happened to the other marsh noises he remembered so well but now no longer heard? Were there still the sounds of rustling wings overhead? Did the little rail still snicker in the tules when he missed a shot? Did the sprig and widgeon still whistle up there? His ears were in their eighties, and the deafness that ran in his family by now had robbed them of much of their hearing. He lived in a far more silent world out there on the marsh.

Still fifteen minutes until shooting time. Despite his deafness he heard a slight splash, looked, and saw a pair of teal had landed among the decoys. They were not comfortable among these unmoving sound-less companions, and in a flurry of departing wings, they left. Shade looked at them, looked at him, and wondered why he did not shoot. They were ducks, weren't they?

Ten minutes. Dawn was backlighting the dark ridges of the Sierra, low on the horizon off to the east, and in the half-light he was beginning to see ducks in flight, black against the lightening sky. Not many ducks, just the occasional pair, sometimes as many as four or five, all out of range.

Five minutes and a courting flight of six sprig, five drakes, and one hen, did their aerial ballet right over the pond and easily in range, oblivious to everything but themselves, dipping, rising, side slipping as they went by. Off in the distance three shots, someone with a fast watch or unable to resist the temptation of a bird in front of them. As if it were a signal to all the rest of the hunters on the marsh, a few more shots, then a barrage as everyone got in the act. Everyone but him, that was. No birds to jump out of the decoy spread for him, none overhead, so he sat back, watched and waited those last minutes until true shooting time.

Not that it mattered, for in those last minutes not a duck came by him, but untold numbers of them obviously were going past other hunt-ers, for the marsh was alive with gunfire, "Crump! Crump! Crump" some 12 gauge spoke, "Pam! Pam!" said some 20 gauge, "Peee-ow-whap!"

---

as someone not far away either ground-sluiced a duck or else tried to finish off a cripple.

Out of the corner of his eye he sensed rather than saw the dog's ears go up as she spotted something airborne, and then drop down again. Following her line of sight, he saw a seagull lazing its way along. This dog was not fooled by a slow flying bird once she saw what it was; she turned away but then her ears perked up again as he too saw the rapid wing beat of something coming at him not fifteen yards up. His ears could not drop the way hers could as he recognized the trailing feet of the mudhen offering his favorite straight overhead shot. He raised the gun to his shoulder, swung smoothly from behind it and out in front, murmuring "Bang" to himself as the mud hen flew on, unaware of what it had just avoided.

Again Shade's ears perked as she gazed eastward, and he quickly picked up on what had caught her attention. A pair of birds coming toward the pond, too far and still too dark to identify by their colors, but by their flight instantly recognizable as shovelers, or "spoonies" as they are called locally. No other duck flies with such reckless, out of control abandon, and he watched as they bored in to the decoys. He decided not to shoot, these birds all too often too fishy tasting from a diet of marine life. He thought about an uncle who had once observed that a fishy spoonie at the table should be accompanied by a white wine, not a red. The two birds made a brief circle and flew off. The dog seemed to have mixed emotions; she didn't like the taste of spoonies if she had to retrieve them, but they were ducks, weren't they?

By now the sound of gunfire had slackened to occasional cr-rRUMPS in the distance, almost all the ducks on the marsh having left for the safety of the bay off to the southwest. He sat back and watched the fiery orange sliver of the edge of the sun peek over the eastern horizon, then become round as it rose, the orange fading as the light increased.

A ripping sound as four ruddy ducks slammed past not three feet above his head, continuing toward the rising sun. Three mudhens came in, landing well outside the decoys but still in range if he wanted mudhens. He didn't.

A quarter hour passed with nothing happening, but then he caught the flicker of white underwing plumage two hundred yards out — a drake mallard looking for a place to set down. He grabbed the duck call on the lanyard around his neck and gave a couple of soft quacks. They reached the greenhead and he responded with his even softer "qua-l-l-ck, qua-i-i-ck" and swung toward the blind, coming low, not ten yards off the water, but still out of range. The hunter rose, his gun to shoulder as the mallard, his wings cupped, made his final approach. The gun spoke once, the duck folded, and the dog broke, splashing out to pick it up and return, bright-eyed, her tail wagging in pride. He said out loud, "We're not skunked!", as his brother would always say after every first bird came to hand when they hunted together. "Good girl, Shade, but you know you shouldn't have broke like that. Go place, girl," and she climbed onto her pad and lay down.

She had barely done so when high above a pair of widgeon started to drop, curved sharp wings making a tearing sound as they came over, went past, and then turned for another look at the decoys. They were still high, but succumbing to his usual fault of taking long-range shots, he stood and pulled the trigger. No response from the trigger; he had forgotten to replace the shell that had killed the mallard. He moved his finger on the rear trigger, but by now the birds had flared, and he knew they were out or range.

Ah well, he thought, you can't get them all, and settled back to search the skies again. By now the sun was well up and it seemed that whatever flight there had been was now over, at least for his corner of the marsh. A few high, very high birds flying in formation passed over him, their disciplined vee formation saying they had no thought at all of coming down to visit his decoys, that they had more distant destinations in mind.

A marsh wren lit upon a dead tule not two feet away from him, inching its way down the dead brown stalk, looking for invisible insects to prey upon, peevishly complaining in its raspy little voice. He froze, watching the wren, but then Shade lifted her head, startling both him and the bird, which flew off.

Shade's ears were cocked again, this time with real interest. He turned to follow her gaze, and in the distance spied a bunch of teal headed past the blind, low but out of range. Hunching down, he squeaked the high-pitched call of a hen, the knot of birds wheeled as if drawn by an invisible string and came back. He rose, led on the first bird, fired, and two teal in the middle angled into the pickleweed twenty yards away.

Hmph, he thought to himself, not doing too well on leading, am I? Again Shade had broken at the shot and was already back with the first bird. He took it from her and told her "Back!" and she was off after the other. This one had had time to hide and it took her a while to pick up its scent. As she tracked on it the little duck swam out into open water, all submerged except for its bill that cut a tell-tale vee on the surface, but she didn't notice. "Shade! Shade!" he shouted, motioning with his hand. Her head came up, she saw the vee in the water, galloped to it and dove her head down, coming up with the teal and returning proudly to the blind.

TEN O'CLOCK AND THREE BIRDS

The sound of shots over the marsh had all but stopped, but one sounded not that far off. He wondered if whoever had fired had connected. More likely yes, maybe a single that went down at the first shot since there were no others. Or, of course, someone bored and frustrated with inactivity had fired just once at some stratospheric bird 80 yards or more in the sky. A Hail Mary shot, as an old hunting companion used to call them.

Club tradition had it that at 9:30 everyone would come in for a big breakfast, but that was one he would break with today; He had some jerky and some dark chocolate to go along with the water he had brought. Sometimes tradition can be ignored.

Another hour crept by and Shade had not once cocked her ears at anything but a few mudhens jerking their way across the pond. His eyes left the duckless sky, and he watched a pair of tiny gossamer spiders at the tip of a tule spear engage in a gargantuan battle to determine who had the right to use it as a launch pad. One finally backed down, and the victor spun out a thread at least a foot long. The hunter wondered what must be going through its mind as it finally let go of the tule and sailed away in the faint breeze. Where did it think it was going?

The mortal combat of the spiders had so grabbed his attention that he failed to notice Shade's ears go forward until she shifted position. He looked up too late to see a courting flight of five pintails, four drakes and a hen, dipping past him within easy range. By the time he grabbed the gun they were out of range, dipping and wheeling like winged ballet dancers. "Well," he thought, "it would not have done to break up that dance, now would it? Better pay more attention."

Again Shade's alarm went off, and this time he caught what she was looking at, four wigeons dropping into his good luck decoys. This time he waited as they made their first swing and then headed in, wings set and feet outstretched. He stood, picked on the lead bird and fired, a quick, clean kill. The other three flared skyward as he swung on the second off to the left. The gun barked its second shot and that bird folded, stone cold dead. This time Shade waited for his release, and when he gave it, shot off her stand like a rocket for the nearer bird, scooping it up and returning, joy in her eyes. She sat, he took the bird, and sent her off for the second. Again she leaped, bounding over the water to bring it back. Two beautiful drakes, the tops of their heads dazzling white, their emerald green cheeks behind the short blue bills. "No wonder they call 'em baldpates," he thought to himself.

Five birds. Should he wait and hope to finish out his limit of seven? No, he decided, no he would not. This had been a good hunt, and there was no need to be greedy. So he pulled himself out of the blind, replaced its cover, retrieved his good luck wigeon decoys, and started the long trudge back to the car. His wife would be glad to have him home early. It had been a *fine* last day.

END NOTES

Pete's brother, Tony Arnold, died on October 8, 2015. Among his papers his family found the following poem. Pete penned a heartfelt reply and I have added my own tribute to one of most noble men I have ever met or hunted with.

— Tom O'Connor

SOME LAST WORDS

Well, yes, I've gone, but it's okay.
You don't know where
But know that I know: there is a There.
It's not Oakland

Death is just a ferryman,
Who draws unearned respect only from the fog
That keeps us from seeing the far shore.
I know.
I've been almost through that fog before,
Close enough to feel a new existence calling.

Once there, can I see back?
Don't know. I think so.
But either way, it's okay.
It really is.

End Notes

Well, yes, I've gone, I'm outward bound.
But parts of me remain.
Not the worn-out body that finally let me down
(Get rid of that — never was much good), but
Maybe a few words, spoken or written,
Will live a while. Hope so.
Just the good ones, of course.
Burn the bad ones, the hurtful ones.
I didn't really mean them.
Mostly.

No, I only live here now
In things I loved so deeply
That I am partly them
And they are partly me:
Launching on an east-coast predawn ebbing tide,
Gurgling swift and black down guzzles to the sea,
Through marshes full of unfilled hunting promise.
Whisper of unseen wings in the dark.
Dawns and sunsets, clouds a preferred option.
Tahoe before anyone else wakes up.
Geese on the Long March,
Calling from on high in the night.
White swans against dark clouds.
All the whistles, chatter, and drunken laughter
Of ducks socializing on an evening feed.
Almost any stink a marsh produces.
The reminder of love in a dog's gentle touch.
A redwood wreath.
Wild strawberries.
These and so many more...

Sense such things and you'll sense me and I'll sense you.

Well, yes, I've gone,
But these parts stay,
And it's okay.
It really is.
I'll see you on the other side.

— *Tony Arnold*

SOME LAST WORDS — A REPLY

Your brother calls to say
Yes, you have gone, but it is not all that okay
We do not know where there is
Or if there is a there, Oakland notwithstanding

But gone you are, beyond our reach,
Suddenly, with so little warning,
On to some nether destination we know not of

Once you almost went beyond that fog hiding that far shore
But got hauled back.
This time you threw off the ties that bound you to us, to this earth
Have you reached that far shore?
Hope so.

So no, it is not really okay
For we can no longer watch you about to say something,
Holding your subject like an invisible basketball — a melon? a boulder?
Weighing it
Between your two hands, lovingly
For you something tangible, maybe visible
That we ourselves cannot feel or see.

End Notes

And it is really not okay that no longer does that
Story of yours — sometimes not all that clean — unfold and as
You hit the punch line, your eyebrows go up,
You pause, and out it comes,
Your close lipped smile, and you looking quizzically at your audience
But it is okay that you left behind that worn out body
And went outward bound as you did
For indeed it let you down these last few years.

And yes, as you wrote, parts of you live here still
In those things you loved so deeply that you noted.
And you live for us in the smell of a redwood wreath
In the taste of a wild strawberry (whose source
You kept secret in that tattered map that showed where they grow,
You guarded it more jealously than any document CIA
Ever entrusted you with).

Now you are in your sacred cathedral
Your ashes around each blind,
So you are one with the pickleweed,
One with the stinky water you loved.

And on the marsh and everywhere
We'll sense you there
And you'll sense us
Just as you said.

So, in all, it has not been all okay
But you are, we hope, safely on the other side
Waiting for us
One day.

— Pete Arnold

ODE FOR TONY

Somewhere out there between adolescence and old age
On near seventy misty mornings a gang of men gathers,
Each new rainy dawn alive with hopeful anticipation,
Each opening day, as yet, a clean and unwritten page.

At the Teal Club quiet voices exchange greetings anew
And laugh at some oft repeated adventure,
A lost companion since last time called to glory,
Smells of gun oil, pipe smoke and the excitement of old Su.

Most are gone now those hunters of times past
But lessons remain of lore and the law
Of hunting ducks and taking care with gun and canoe
Of leading right when they come in high and fast.

When it comes to me the smell of marshes in the rain
I feel a cold cruel wind full of promise and snow
At the club house a fire glows and glass of something warmer
And for just a moment we are young and free again.

In the thickets the year has again turned the leaves
Sitting inside by my fire full of sleep and only half aware
Of the rain tapping a message on my window pane
And the wind whispering to me from under the eaves.

I hear again Tony's quiet laugh and see a dawn through branches bare,
Eyes scanning the darkened sky waiting for opening time
Then at last to make ready and finally load the gun
I like to think they gather with him still somewhere out there.

— *Tom O'Connor*

CPSIA information can be obtained
at www.ICGtesting.com
Printed in the USA
LVHW080349290622
722374LV00007B/123

9 780578 682853